This book is for the students who
pray, learn, serve, gather, and lead
at the Sheil Catholic Center
at Northwestern University.

You are my teachers and my inspiration.

Mary Deeley (M.Div, Yale Divinity School; PhD., Northwestern University) is passionate about talking with people about where they find God in their lives. Mary received an early degree in music that turned into an abiding love for ministry and Scripture. She has taught, worked, and ministered in academic settings since 1978. Currently, Mary serves as the pastoral associate and director of Christ the Teacher Institute for the Sheil Catholic Center at Northwestern University, where she works with young adults and others in discernment processes, leadership development, spiritual direction, and education and formation.

Acknowledgments

I honestly didn't know I would be writing a first book, let alone a second, so I am as surprised as anyone. But I am also extraordinarily grateful to the many individuals who supported and encouraged me throughout this process.

Thanks to my husband, Dan, and daughters, Katy and Annie, who are God's gift to me in good times and bad, fiercely loyal, loving, and challenging in varied and good ways.

Thanks to Rachel and Alexis, who read chapters and gave me feedback in the midst of busy lives and who have bridged the gap from being students to being friends with grace and humor. Thanks as well to Debbie, Beth, and Cindy, who read the first book and were still willing to look at the second. They are dear companions to whom I owe dinner and more.

I am very grateful for the Sheil family—students, associates, and staff—who encouraged me in my writing and to all those who, when I described the book, said, "I think I need to read that book."

I want to thank the good people at Liguori Press, especially Father Mat and Christy, who invited the second book and more.

And finally, to my guides, mentors, and friends in the spiritual life—Ken, Dave, and Paul. We've been through interesting times; thanks for always being there.

Remembering GOD

RESTING IN THE MIDST OF LIFE

Mary Katharine Deeley

To Mary
Dear friend, may your
memories of God guide &
protect you always.
Peace
Mary

Liguori
Liguori, Missouri

Imprimi Potest:
Harry Grile, CSsR, Provincial
Denver Province, The Redemptorists

Published by Liguori Publications
Liguori, Missouri 63057

To order, call 800-325-9521
www.liguori.org

Library of Congress Cataloging-in-Publication Data

Deeley, Mary Katharine.
Remembering God : resting in the midst of life / Mary Katharine Deeley.
-- 1st ed.
p. cm.
1. Spiritual life--Catholic Church. 2. Spirituality--Catholic Church.
I. Title.
BX2350.3.D43 2012
248.4'82--dc23
2012026494

pISBN: 978-0-7648-2169-1
eISBN: 978-0-7648-2318-3

Liguori Publications, a nonprofit corporation, is an apostolate of The Redemptorists. To learn more about The Redemptorists, visit Redemptorists.com.

Printed in the United States of America
16 15 14 13 12 / 5 4 3 2 1
First Edition

Contents

Introduction

The student leaned against the doorjamb of my office and sighed audibly. Ever the astute minister, I asked what was going on, and she said, "I don't know what I'm going to do." She was at the beginning of her senior year, three years of coursework into her major, and she had just realized she didn't really want to go into the field she had chosen. The more she talked, the more anxiety showed on her face as she considered her options—change majors and take longer to graduate, finish the major and graduate but find a job in some other field, finish and do some volunteer work for a couple of years until she figured out what she wanted to do. They were all viable options with pros and cons. None stood out as the best or worst, and at one point she simply sighed again and said, "I've been thinking about this for a long time and I just don't want to think about it anymore. I know I need to make a decision, but right now I just need some quiet space in my head and in my heart."

We went on to talk about some other things that were happening for her, but that last sentence stayed with me. Don't we all need a little bit of quiet space at certain moments of our lives where we can put decision-making on the back burner, at least for a while, and stop agonizing over the major questions (or even the little ones) and life choices? It's not that the decisions aren't important or the questions shouldn't be considered carefully; it's that decisions made from a place of anxiety, worry, and busyness are rarely free, peaceful, or joyful. Unfortunately, we live in a world that tells us more often than not that "who we are" is intricately bound to the job we have and where we live. The voice of friends and family and our own interior voice urge us to make decisions that will determine our path for years to come so that we will not "waste time" doing things that seem to have no bearing on our future. No wonder the student stood in my office door and sighed. She felt she had let everyone down, including herself.

But at the heart of Christian belief is a God who knows who we are and calls us by name to an abundant life that is not bound by the job we have, the money we earn, or the car we drive. This God calls us to a place where we can make our choices out of trust, even when we are not certain; out of freedom, not out of obligation; and as a response to God's love and grace rather than our own fear and need.

Sometimes, though, we get so caught up in the process of trying to find answers to our questions that we lose sight of the foundations that anchor our search. We forget that we need to rest every now and then. And we forget *how* to rest in the midst of everything else that is going on. In a busy and noisy world, the very notion of rest and quiet fills some with dread. Students going on retreat are often stunned when we ask them to turn off cell phones and try to resist a computer. We become attached to noisemakers like TV and MP3 players, and we can rarely think of going anywhere without our cell phone. There is hardly a moment in which we can breathe in the quiet and find ourselves simply waiting for the next move, confident that it will come and ready when it does. This is true in our work, in our relationships, and in our desire to grow more deeply in God.

Finding the resting point does not mean giving up altogether and forgetting the questions or finding a way to procrastinate until the decision is made for us. Rather, it is finding the point in which we can re-center ourselves and from which we can move in any direction. Dancers, mime artists, yoga practitioners, and even military personnel are familiar with the term, if not in words, then in their bodies. The military position "at ease," the first position for dancers, neutral points for mime and yoga, and even the stance of football players before the snap are all places of attentive restfulness. In them, we prepare ourselves to move, quickly and confidently, in any direction. Thus the ballerina creates the dance, the yoga practitioner disciplines the body, and the football player moves into the play. In the spiritual life, the resting point helps us recover our sense of self, discover things we did not know, and *remember what God has had to say to us all along.* We stand "at ease" in the face of questions that remain unanswered and lives that remain complicated so that we can move out again in joy and freedom.

To get to that spiritual "resting point," we need two things: time and memory. We need time, that is, a willingness to enter the present and stay there rather than look to the future. And memory helps us bring the stories of God's relationship with us into the present. Perhaps more to the point, we need the *time* to *remember* the stories of God with us. I love the thought of taking *time* and the significance of the word *memory.* To remember is to put something back together again. When we remember, we make present the beginning when different decisions can be made and different emotions come to the fore. Certainly, it can be difficult in the middle of the complexities of life to imagine taking a little time off from the process of decision-making to embrace the process of remembering. But when we remember who God is and how God has worked in our lives and in the lives of others, we can find our "resting point," and from there we can embrace the love, trust, and freedom we need to make the decisions and live the grace-filled lives that lie before us. From this resting point, we can move in any direction and know that God walks with us wherever we go.

I was only vaguely aware of how much we need these resting points until I went on retreat a few years ago. There I was engaged in the things we do when the questions of our lives begin to crowd in, weigh us down, or just demand a little more of our attention. I worried, I overthought issues. I felt in my whole being what that long-ago student had voiced: "I just need some quiet space."

Two things came to me simultaneously. The first was a snippet from *The Four Quartets* by T.S. Eliot on exploration and the journey. Eliot indicates that when our journey ends, we will recognize for the very first time our genesis, our starting place. I realized this was true, but at that moment, it was not all that comforting. I wanted to make some decisions; I did not want to be in the same place when I returned to my home and work.

The second thought was that we are pilgrims who come from and will eventually go home to God. We are on a pilgrimage even now, but our vision isn't 20/20 at this point. Saint Paul wrote that we see God dimly, as though in a mirror; at the end, we shall see God face-to-face (1 Corinthians 13:12). It is so close in spirit to what Eliot wrote that I think Eliot may have been channeling Paul just a little. These two thoughts created a movement in my mind and heart—into a consideration of how I see God now, even if it's just a dim vision, and away from questions such as, "Who am I, and what am I going to do now?" Scriptures, stories, and my own experience came and went from my mind until a different question emerged, "What does God know that I don't?" This question was a divinely inspired invitation to find my own "resting point." Here I realized that if I took the time to reflect on and remember what God knows, then I might just discover where I can find my bearings and the grace to keep going—and in the end, God willing, I would recognize what I've been looking for all along.

Remembering God—what God knows about us and the world, who God is for us and the world—grounds us in our foundation and brings us to attentive restfulness. In memory, we can know the presence of the Divine in the midst of confusion. Whether we call it a resting point, neutral position, safe harbor, oasis, sanctuary, refuge, or lesson on the way, these metaphors help us grasp the same reality. We have entered sacred time and space in which our decisions, whether different or similar to what we first expected, come out of the freedom, joy, and peace that befits a child of God. Here we can be confident that God accompanies us and has brought us this far by faith and grace and that the Lord will not leave us orphans or abandon us to our own devices. Indeed, we have been standing on holy ground this whole time, and God has just been waiting for us to step aside and listen.

Remembering God is an invitation to find spiritual "resting points" for the many questions of our lives. The stories and meditations in this book are drawn from our common heritage in Scripture and particular life stories. In them we will discover what God knows that we often forget. We will find moments of rest and positions of quiet attentiveness that will give us time to reset and then return a little more refreshed and less anxious to the messy business of living. By taking time to rest and remember God, we can return to our noisy and busy lives ready to engage our questions with an awakened sense of possibility for our lives.

This book is for that long-ago student who filled my doorway and for the countless women and men who become anxious and worried because they face too many decisions or have too few possibilities and not nearly enough time or space to consider any of this every day. This is not a book about answers, or even how to find the answers; it is an invitation to remember, rest, and leave refreshed. May you find it helpful on your path to God.

Part I

Remembering God When We Wonder Who We Are

"Who are you?" said the Caterpillar.
Alice replied rather shyly,
"I—I hardly know, sir, just at present—
at least I know who I was when I got up this morning,
but I think I must have been changed several times since then."

Lewis Carroll, *Alice's Adventures in Wonderland*

Chapter 1

God Has Always Known Who You Are

The Question: Who Am I?

What's your name? Where are you from? What is your major? These three questions form about 95 percent of the conversations in the first week of a student's freshman year at college. With some variation, the pattern is repeated when someone moves to a new town, starts a new job, or simply goes to relax at the local watering hole. There we might substitute, "What do you do?" or in Chicago, "Cubs or Sox?" One student got so tired of answering the questions that he wore a nametag that said simply: Matt, Houston, Chemistry.

All over campus in that first week and beyond, people explore new ways of asking and answering questions that will reveal a little more of who someone is beyond the "name, rank, and serial number" mentality. Sometimes the variations are subtle but effective: "Where's home for you? What's keeping you busiest these days? What should I know?" All of these are in service to an unarticulated but important understanding: Who we are is not just what we do or where we are from. Our name identifies family, culture, and sometimes generation. Then we move on to so much more—sense of humor, ways of expressing ourselves, the roles we play, what we like to do in our spare time, the books we read, the songs we sing, the faith we practice (or don't), and what we want to be in the future.

In the great "let's pretend" of childhood, we try on different characters and imagine being doctors, paleontologists (one of the perennial favorites), volcanologists, firefighters, princesses, teachers, priests, nurses, mothers, and fathers. Some of these roles feel comfortable for years; others for about a minute and a half. During our childhood and teen years, we put on and take off these identities without a second thought as we grow into our own talents and abilities. Besides these rehearsals for "what we will be when we grow up," there are also the multiple identities we acquire by the time we turn eighteen. We are daughters and sons, friends, employees, students, and acquaintances. Each of these carries its own set of priorities, joys, and challenges, and we have to learn to juggle them all. It's little wonder that the question "Who am I today?" takes on a good deal of significance as we think about career paths, places to live, and our own integrity as adults.

As we approach adulthood, however, the question becomes more insistent, aided by well-meaning parents, friends, and teachers. "You are so good at that...Of course, you want to go into the family business...Don't you want to be a...?" Everything—from our names to our childhood imaginations to the roles we now play to what we wish for ourselves and what others wish for us—gives us a snapshot of our identity, but it's never the whole of it.

Is it any wonder, then, that in moments of transition, stress, or transforming events, our grasp of who we are can alter and shift until we, like Alice, recognize that we have changed many times since we got up in the morning. The first time most of us experience such a transition is when we move out of our parents' house and into our own, whether that is a dorm room, apartment, or rooming house. We are always their children, but who are we apart from our parents? What do we want to do and where do we want to go? Frequently the response is to experiment with schedules, rules, and varying degrees of responsibility from going to class to holding down a job.

Sometimes the change is so extreme that we surprise both our friends and ourselves. One freshman I encountered, in an effort to find his identity in a particular fraternity, started partying and drinking heavily. When he came to me, he was feeling a disconnect between what he was doing and what he enjoyed. He commented, “This is so different than who I was. I don’t know myself right now.” The concept troubled him greatly. We talked over many weeks about how he would describe himself and what priorities he wanted to set regarding actions consistent with who he said he was and, truth be told, who he wanted to be.

In the midst of that long conversation, he said he’d gone home for a couple of weekends “to reconnect with my parents.” Even now as I remember his words, I realize he went back to reconnect not only with his parents, but with a time when he knew more clearly who he was. He went to take a breather from his questions and his doubts. And there at home he found a resting point. It was temporary, to be sure, but it provided something he was looking for: that particular place of balance where he could remember who he was, where he came from, and what was important to him. The visits calmed him and helped him find the strength to move forward to the next step.

The transition moments of our lives affect our sense of who we are, and that makes it hard to get our bearings in unfamiliar territory. At that point, we come face-to-face with one of the deep desires of our hearts—to be known fully with all our beauty and all our flaws and to be loved precisely because we have this unique combination of both. We want someone who knows us so well that when we lose ourselves or forget who we are and what is important to us, he or she can hold up the mirror that reflects back to us the priorities of our hearts and helps us find the right path. These are the people to whom we need to make no explanation; rather, they nod their heads in delight when we are our truest selves and become a beacon for us when we go astray. They are not afraid to jog our memories or slap the back of our heads when we get it wrong. These are the people who help us see what we cannot and keep us from taking ourselves too seriously.

As Alice discovered, keeping up with who we are is hard work. Being honest about where we do it well and where we could do it better is even more difficult. But when we are able simply to stop and listen, it is our grace to encounter the deep and abiding understanding that who we are and always will be was present in us from the beginning. Indeed, the heart of who we are does not change. We may lose sight of that from time to time, but God, who created us, never does. Put another way: the certainty of who we are is best answered through understanding *whose* we are. As children of God, in a relationship of love with God, we are already everything we can be. When we remember that, we can move in any direction with confidence. We have found our "resting point."

The Resting Point: The Memory That God Knows Who You Are

Meditate and pray through the memory using the following Scripture passages, and recall the God who *formed your inmost being.* Take your time and read the Scriptures aloud. Enhance your resting place by letting the meditation carry you into the prayer.

[O Lord] You formed my inmost being;
    you knit me in my mother's womb.
I praise you, because I am wonderfully made;
    wonderful are your works!
My very self you know.
My bones are not hidden from you,
When I was being made in secret,
    fashioned in the depths of the earth.
Your eyes saw me unformed;
    in your book all are written down;
    my days were shaped, before one came to be.

Psalm 139:13–16

Pause for Meditation

I once had a spiritual director who suggested I pray this psalm every day for a month and continually invite God to reveal what God knew about me. Every day I reflected on the fact that God knew my thoughts, my *going out and my coming in*, and most of all, that God had known me from the very beginning of my being. "What do you know about me?" I asked, pleaded, prayed. Occasionally good times and good acts would come to mind—places and situations in which I had done my best and both God and I knew it. At other moments (and there were far more of these), the places, times, and relationships where I had missed the mark were a bit more evident. I wasn't sure whether it was good or bad that God knew me so well. Certainly, I thought, there were issues better left undiscussed. I shared many of these findings with my director, who said, "God knows all that and created you anyway and continues to be with you even today. What do you make of that?"

I was caught. In a moment of insight, I realized that the mystery of who I was and who I was becoming was not a mystery to God. I could only stand in profound awe that God could know me that well and not turn away. The psalmist asks, "Where can I go from your spirit? From your presence, where can I flee?" (139:7). In truth, as long as we carry ourselves with us, there is no place we can go that God does not know us. We can change jobs, move far away, or start new lives as couples or on our own. We can try to erase the past or refuse to talk about it, good or bad, and God still knows the whole of it. That may be uncomfortable at times. But the thought of such faithfulness means we are in it—God and us—for the long haul. And in a way, it makes the journey easier.

For some, the thought that God knows us better than we know ourselves might suggest predestination. This is not so. Predestination suggests that God sets things in motion and walks away, knowing what will happen and therefore not needing to pay it any attention. Psalm 139 talks about God knowing us so well that he knows how we will finish a sentence or react to a given set of circumstances sometimes before we do. But rather than walk away, God uses the knowledge to gently steer us toward a slightly different course if we go astray. More important, God knows the *possibility* of us. God already sees the gift we can be when we are fully open to grace, and God invites us to live into that possibility, rejoicing over every step that takes us closer, no matter how small it may seem to us. The whole of Psalm 139 is an acknowledgment and a praise of God's universal presence and the impossibility of finding a place where God is not. I think this is why the psalm is a favorite of so many, and one of mine as well.

Prayer Action

Begin by praying the scriptural verse aloud and then pause, allowing your heart as well as your mind to hear the words deeply. When you are ready, read the reflection following each Scripture slowly.

LORD, you have probed me, you know me:
you know when I sit and stand;
you understand my thoughts from afar....
Even before a word is on my tongue,
LORD, you know it all.

PSALM 139:1–2, 4

Simply become aware of your body and its position. Let your thoughts come uncensored to your mind. God holds you no matter what position your body adopts. God is mindful of your peace and anxiety, your worries and your joys. Whatever is on your mind, God is capable of hearing it and keeping it close. Speak the first words that come to you. Know that God hears both the outward word and any of its hidden meanings. God knows your heart and what lies hidden there, both what you choose to reveal and what you do not. Lay your questions down and rest, confident that you do not have to find words for them now. This is an invitation.

Behind and before you encircle me
and rest your hand upon me....
Where can I go from your spirit?
From your presence, where can I flee?
If I ascend to the heavens, you are there;
if I lie down in Sheol, there you are....
If I say, "Surely darkness shall hide me,
and night shall be my light"—
Darkness is not dark for you,
and night shines as the day.
Darkness and light are but one.

PSALM 139:5, 7–8, 11–12

We live our lives in linear fashion with beginnings and endings. But God is behind and before us. There is no past or future, here or there in which God is not present. And in many ways, God lays a divine hand on us, though we may not know it at the time. Whether we feel so close to God that we can say we live where God lives or we feel so isolated that we say we might as well be dead (Sheol was the realm of the dead), the psalmist declares that God is there and holds us fast. God does not force; God never forces. God waits with us and for us until we can recognize ourselves as beloved by God. And even in those periods of darkness (and we have all had them—sometimes so profoundly dark that we cannot find the way out without help), God sees who we are. Even if we lose ourselves, God will not lose us.

You formed my inmost being;
you knit me in my mother's womb.
I praise you, because I am wonderfully made;
wonderful are your works!
My very self you know.
My bones are not hidden from you,
When I was being made in secret,
fashioned in the depths of the earth.
Your eyes saw me unformed;
in your book all are written down;
my days were shaped, before one came to be.

God knows us from the inside out. For some of us, this may be more of a cause for dismay than for celebration. If God knows everything, then God has seen the very best we have to offer and the very worst of which we are capable, both of which take up residence in our hearts and minds on occasion. For the psalmist, though, God's knowledge is an occasion of freedom and a chance to remember that we can make different choices in how we live the life we have been given. God has more designs for us than we can count. That means we have done, thought, felt, or said nothing that God cannot use to bring us closer to him, because God knows us better than we know ourselves. Our possibilities are held safely in the heart of God.

The word of the Lord came to me:
Before I formed you in the womb I knew you,
    before you were born I dedicated you,
    a prophet to the nations I appointed you.
"Ah, Lord God!" I said,
    "I do not know how to speak; I am too young!"
But the Lord answered me,
Do not say, "I am too young."
    To whomever I send you, you shall go;
    whatever I command you, you shall speak.
Do not be afraid of them,
    for I am with you to deliver you — oracle of the Lord.

Jeremiah 1:4–8

Pause for Meditation

A young couple mourning the death of their infant chose this reading from Jeremiah for the funeral Mass. When I asked them about it, they expressed their faith that God had been with their child from the beginning and that the child had fulfilled the role God had wanted for him even though his life had been so short. The remark stayed with me. God *knows* how to work through us even when we are young in spite of our assessment of our own weaknesses and inabilities and because of his love for us. More significantly, God doesn't just know how to do this, God *chooses* to work through us in particular ways, guiding our steps in the life to which he has called us. And God manifests the confidence that we will do as he asks. Evoking one of the great comforting phrases of Scripture, we recall that God says, *Do not be afraid of them.*

Frequently, our fear either paralyzes us and keeps us from making decisions or goads us into making the wrong decision. But here is a wonderful understanding. God is with us whatever path we follow; God can make the best of all our decisions. Reconnecting with this understanding of God can give us firm ground for a life that abounds with questions and with paths that are less than clear.

Prayer Action

Begin by praying the scriptural verse aloud and then pause, allowing your heart as well as your mind to hear the words. When you are ready, read the reflection following each Scripture slowly.

> *The word of the Lord came to me:*
> *Before I formed you in the womb I knew you...*

Before we came to be, God already knew us. God held us in the divine mind and heart, waiting for the right moment to shape us into being and breathe life into us. What is the nature of God's knowing? We may never be able to answer that question, but we are confronted with the reality of God's knowing before we knew ourselves. In this, we understand something else: God's knowing is timeless, it did not begin with us; rather, in it we had our beginning. What does this have to do with the creative power of God's love? What God loves, God knows, from the tiniest invertebrate to the very image of God: the human person. God's love permeates our inmost being and assures us that God is with us, even when we are just a gleam in his eye.

...before you were born I dedicated you,
a prophet to the nations I appointed you.

To dedicate is to set aside or to commit someone or something for a unique purpose. God set Jeremiah aside to be a prophet to the nations—to call them to faithfulness to the Law and point to where God was working in the world. We, too, were dedicated by God for a purpose or purposes we may not yet know. Our purpose is not necessarily the same as our job or our role. Instead, God works through us to accomplish his purpose by guiding us to roles, careers, and self-understanding that allow us to open ourselves to God. Jeremiah simply acknowledges that God does this from the first moment we are created. It makes sense. In that moment, we are most open to the grace of God, and let's face it, grace wants a head start before we are influenced too readily by the world.

"Ah, Lord GOD!" I said,
"I do not know how to speak; I am too young!"
But the LORD answered me,
Do not say, "I am too young."
To whomever I send you, you shall go;
whatever I command you, you shall speak.
Do not be afraid of them,
for I am with you to deliver you—oracle of the LORD.

Too young, too old, not smart enough, not good enough—these are some of the many messages that fill our minds when we are wrestling with the question of who we are. Saint Ignatius would say this is the work of the evil one, and I would tend to agree. If we are not good enough, it doesn't matter who we are. God does not deny the imperfection; rather, he substitutes a mantra for the one in our head: "Do not be afraid." We have forgotten that God knows what our challenges are and what we will have to overcome to serve his will. Just as God is with us and knows us from the womb, God will be with us and know us throughout our lives. Such knowledge is the source of God's remarkable confidence in so fragile a people. It is also the answer to our deep desire—to be fully known, loved, and believed in for who we are.

A Prayer for Those Who Wonder Who They Are

Good and gracious Lord,
I am in trouble and I find myself saying more and more,
"This is not who I am."

Who I am seems to have gotten lost in the challenge of living;
I am playing at whatever I think
everyone else wants me to be.

But in the midst of it all, I do not know who I am;
and I am tired—
tired of asking the questions and looking for the answers.

So grant me grace, Lord,
to remember that you called me
your child from the beginning.

Let me remember that you are already working through me.

And let me remember that you hold the possibilities
for what I will become in your hand.

Give me the confidence to know that you will never let me go,
never forget who you called me to be.

In you, I will find my truest self.

Amen.

Chapter 2

God Encourages Change

The Question: Why Aren't Things the Way They Used to Be?

Someone once said that if we want to make God laugh, we should tell him our plans. I don't know if that's true (though I think God does have a sense of humor), but I have certainly been surprised (and *surprised* is a kind word) a few times in my life for both the good and not-so-good things that have happened to me. On more than one occasion, I have picked myself up and shook my head in wonder at the strange ways in which my life has worked out. *What could God possibly have had in mind in* this *situation?* The truth, though, is that our lives, however short or long, privileged or poverty-stricken, are measured in the changes that come our way. Simply getting older changes our bodies; books, newspapers, education, and conversation change our minds; and the people we encounter from day to day change our hearts. The changes might propel us into a new and better direction or they might throw us for a loop, but we cannot prevent them from happening.

Sometimes I imagine that we go through our days guarding our habits, memories, and images of who we are like treasures. We cannot bear to part with them, for they move when we do, even if something better comes along. In my house, we moved my college textbooks three times before I decided I could part with them. In three moves, they were never once taken out of the box. And they were just books, the remnants of a younger life. I have clung to some habits and ways of thinking much longer, and it's much harder to get rid of those. Trying to do so, for all of us, often produces anxiety and stress. But clinging to "the way things used to be" is not always the best way to grow. On the contrary, if we take the time to change minds and hearts, leaving behind the old self and putting on the new, it shapes the way we look at the world and forms us into the people we are becoming.

Where do we find the challenges to change? These challenges occur particularly in moments of transition when we lose our balance. Leaving our childhood and taking our place as adults is one such moment. We can also find these challenges in the "aha" moments when we at last realize what it is we really want to do. The death of a family member or friend can be a third. Transition moments are cusp moments. Here we come face-to-face with decisions and movement that feel more like leaps of faith than anything else. These are the times we pray for grace, bless (or curse) the situation, ask for help, and sometimes assail heaven and earth to move us into a more stable period. We feel out of kilter and disoriented. The phrases we use in these times come easily: "I didn't know which end was up"; "I felt like I was at sea"; "I just wanted it to stop."

One unsettling reality of change is that it reminds us that we are not on stable ground, nor are we finished quite yet. The shifts and turns in our lives—and we can sometimes think of them as earthquakes—force us to think differently and to switch perspectives. We can respond well or badly, we can make our way forward or decide to sit stubborn and unmoving, but we cannot deny that change is happening and is nearly a constant. If we don't get rid of some of the baggage we've been carrying around, it becomes very hard to move to solid ground. The other unsettling notion is the realization that God encourages change in our minds, hearts, and lives. The creative love of God manifests itself in growth and life. We cannot grow if we do not change. The Scriptures tell us that we are a new creation in Christ. If we are able to let go of whatever it is we have been holding on to, then we can make enough room to see the grace inherent in moments of change. We might even be surprised by the outcome.

When I taught in the seminary, I sat on the admissions committee. We all took turns interviewing students. I always enjoyed getting to know the students as we probed their reasons for wanting to be ordained. My favorite part of the interview was listening to prospective seminarians tell the story of being called to priesthood. Although each story was unique in its details, similarities abounded. One theme seemed to weave into everyone's story: They heard the call of God to ministry—and ignored it, sometimes for years. The excuses were varied: "I was sure God was joking," or "I wasn't ready to leave my life." They finished school, took jobs, and kept hearing a persistent voice that kept them up at night. Finally they could no longer keep it at bay and left the life they had known to come to seminary and prepare for a different kind of work. One seminarian said, "No one was more surprised than me. If someone had told me ten years ago that this was where I was headed, I would not have believed them." He paused briefly and then continued, "I never considered myself a particularly religious person, but I find myself excited to talk about God and church to others. I want to listen to them talk about God in their lives." The call to seminary for a "not particularly religious" person was an earthquake—a shift in perspective that threw him out of balance; the discovery of gifts and a passion he didn't know before made for more solid ground. God encouraged it all.

It strikes me that God and God's grace find us where we are in the pathways of our lives: joyful, sorrowful, wandering, weak, earnest, searching. And God's grace "unbalances" us so that we might see a new perspective and come to a new part of the path. Remembering that God encourages change in us and brings us to growth just might create the anticipation and eagerness that opens us up to God's presence and allows us to let go of whatever has been keeping our options limited. That is our resting point.

The Resting Point: The Memory That God Encourages Change

Meditate and pray through the memory using the following Scripture passages, and recall that God *accompanies you through moments of transition.* Take your time and read the Scriptures aloud. Enhance your resting place by letting the meditation carry you into the prayer.

> That night, however, Jacob arose, took his two wives, with the two maidservants and his eleven children, and crossed the ford of the Jabbok. After he got them and brought them across the wadi and brought over what belonged to him, Jacob was left there alone. Then a man wrestled with him until the break of dawn. When the man saw that he could not prevail over him, he struck Jacob's hip at its socket, so that Jacob's socket was dislocated as he wrestled with him. The man then said, "Let me go, for it is daybreak." But Jacob said, "I will not let you go until you bless me." "What is your name?" the man asked. He answered, "Jacob." Then the man said, "You shall no longer be named Jacob, but Israel, because you have contended with divine and human

> beings and have prevailed." Jacob then asked him, "Please tell me your name." He answered, "Why do you ask for my name?" With that, he blessed him. Jacob named the place Peniel, "because I have seen God face to face," he said, "yet my life has been spared."
>
> GENESIS 32:23–31

Pause for Meditation

It was fitting that Jacob wrestled at night, mainly because the dark seems made for wrestling with all kinds of things. In the Trappist Abbey I visit, a short description of the Liturgy of the Hours explains that the prayer known as Vigils (3:30 AM) is one of the longer prayers because people who are facing difficult changes in their lives and are troubled, anxious, and lonely are often wakeful in the dark, unable to find their rest in sleep. The monks make it part of their ministry to keep watch with and pray for those who are struggling or for whom the words of prayer do not come easily. No one who has read that explanation has failed to grasp the compassion and comfort displayed in the solidarity the monks show. Can they directly help those in trouble? No, at least not in the way we think about it. But if we believe what our faith and our Lord tell us—that God does hear prayer and does intervene in our lives—then the prayer of the monks makes all the sense in the world. And those of us who worry and wonder how we will make it through the dark places of our lives can have confidence that there are groups of men and women who keep vigil with us and raise their voices in prayer even when we cannot.

Jacob might have appreciated the monks' compassion. On his journey with his family and possessions, he heard that his brother, Esau, the same one whom Jacob had cheated of his birthright, was coming to meet him. The questions must have weighed heavily on him. *Have things changed between us? Does he hate me? Can he forgive me? Will he kill me on sight?* And perhaps Jacob was clinging to some of his own guilt or self-righteousness as well. All of those things took shape in a man (some say it was an angel) who wrestles with Jacob throughout the night and until the break of day. Our worries may not take human form, but we wrestle just the same, wakeful and watchful and fearful of the change that is happening when the cares of life, our own questions, and the worry of broken relationships and situations press down upon us.

But here is the interesting part. Jacob recognizes that God is somehow present in the wrestling. He may be off balance, but he understands, for he says, "I have seen God face to face, and I am still alive." Later in the story, Jacob sees Esau, who embraces him in love and kindness rather than in anger. Jacob says in wonder, "Seeing you is like seeing the face of God." The unexpected gift of forgiveness gave Jacob a new perspective and brought him to solid ground. I wonder if Jacob would have been so open to seeing the love in his brother's eyes if he had not first had to wrestle all night. The emotional and mental strength he needed to hang on to the fear, and perhaps even hatred, of his brother was spent in his midnight bout. Perhaps the limp was a reminder that stubborn patterns of thought and behavior prevent change.

I believe that God sometimes wrestles with us to challenge our resistance, our fear of the unknown, and our certainty that we know the outcome. Furthermore, he wrestles with us to support and strengthen us when we face our own inconsistency, stubbornness, or inability to let go of our cherished habits of mind and heart. In any case and in whatever way possible, God does not just encourage our change; he promotes it with patient pursuit, with periodic movement, and with the occasional all-night struggle. We cannot always anticipate when it will happen, but we can be found ready when it does.

Prayer Action

Change is what happens when things don't go the way we thought they would or as we planned. Pray the story of Jacob aloud, and then find a comfortable position and place in which you can spend some time remembering. Call to mind and heart the last time you wrestled with a change you needed to make. Reflect on these questions for as long as you are able: What invited (or forced) the change? What were your questions? What were you afraid of? What (or whom) did you wrestle with in the dark? What was the blessing you asked for and received (you may still be waiting to know)? What is the mark of your encounter? In all of this, where was God (though the answer might be, "I don't see him yet")?

Now reflect on those dear friends, mentors, and guides whom God has put in your life. Who has reflected the face of God to you? Who has provided the unexpected gift and the nudge to see things differently? What change do you see in yourself as a result of these encounters?

When you have finished your reflection, read the story of Jacob again (and continue into the next chapter if you'd like to read his encounter with Esau to hear Jacob say, "To see your face is for me like seeing the face of God"). Give thanks for God's work in your life, whether he has wrestled with you to get you to let go of the old self or wrestled in support of you and against the evil of the world. Know that God encourages your growth into his life and welcomes any change that brings you closer to him. Find your resting point as you prepare to move into the world again, and close with a prayer of your choosing.

But now, thus says the LORD,
    who created you, Jacob, and formed you, Israel:
Do not fear, for I have redeemed you;
    I have called you by name: you are mine.
When you pass through waters, I will be with you;
    through rivers, you shall not be swept away.
When you walk through fire, you shall not be burned,
    nor will flames consume you.
For I, the LORD, am your God,
    the Holy One of Israel, your savior.
I give Egypt as ransom for you,
    Ethiopia and Seba in exchange for you.
Because you are precious in my eyes
    and honored, and I love you,
I give people in return for you
    and nations in exchange for your life.

ISAIAH 43:1–4

Pause for Meditation

Isaiah's poetic rendering of God's message to Israel is like balm to a people who have wondered if God abandoned them in their sin. The exile to Babylon could not have come as anything but an unwelcome and unexpected development to those who felt God was on their side. And yet God entered into that change and into the consciousness of Israel to claim love for the people and the pledge of protection in the disasters of life. "Do not fear," the familiar message goes. Neither flood nor fire will take us away from God's love. In his Letter to the Romans many centuries later, Saint Paul would echo those sentiments, saying that nothing "will be able to separate us from the love of God" (8:39). Isaiah's most significant line, though, comes toward the end: "You are precious in my eyes and honored, and I love you" (43:4).

In many of the great myths of the world, the gods regard human beings as insignificant playthings, but here in the Hebrew and Christian Scriptures, we find that God loves us—enough to walk with us through an imperfect world and an imperfect life. He loves us enough to be present in our greatest joy and in our deepest hour of darkness. God loves us enough to show up when we are wrestling and mark us as his own with grace and a name and a little limp, just so we don't forget who's who. When we begin to grasp this amazing truth, we suddenly realize that grace abounds in our lives. We are forgiven and we learn how to forgive. We find joy in grief and peace in times of war. We learn that there is nothing so evil in us or others that God cannot transform if we are open to the miracle of it and believe with all our hearts that God can make a difference in us.

This is not "pie in the sky" talk or wishful thinking. It is being able to hold in heart and mind two realities at once: that we are human and imperfect and that we have been given the amazing gift of eternal life in Jesus Christ, who has promised to be with us always. We are stubborn and unreceptive to change, but we can come to sudden clarity that we are redeemed and called by name to the grace of God, who changes us more than we can say. When a change of fortune or circumstance (for good or bad) overwhelms us, remember God's glorious words to his people. From that resting point we can move in any direction, for the Lord is with us.

Prayer Action

Find a comfortable place and position and slowly reread this passage from Isaiah aloud. Choose one line from the passage as a constant refrain. Pray that line over and over for two or three minutes, and then slowly begin to lay before God everything that is unsettling or throws you off balance. If it helps, write them down or speak them aloud. After each thing named, repeat your chosen phrase. (For example, I might name a distressing situation with a family member and say, "When you pass through the waters, I will be with you.") Open yourself to the presence of God as much as possible. Watch carefully for the places in which God stands beside you, offering his strength through the days or weeks of change. Listen as God reveals his presence in your heart, and humbly ask him for the grace to embrace the conversion and transformation that give you a new perspective.

When you have remembered everything you can, give thanks for the grace of God's creative love, without which we would never grow. Give thanks for his presence with you in the times of hard change and easy transitions. Offer your life to God as an instrument of his love so that you might be an example and a guide for others.

A Prayer for Those Who Wonder Why Things Can't Stay the Same

Dear Lord,
I don't always like surprises,
and change sometimes comes hard for me.

I wonder if I am cut out for this life
or if I should look for something else.

Give me the grace to remember
that I am glorious in your sight
and that you love me.

But even more, give me the grace to believe it
so that believing I might go into the unknown
with the anticipation that you are already there
even as you walk with me here.

Help me remember that in the midst of my changing,
you will be constant,
wrestling with my reluctance
when I don't want to go to a new place
and wrestling with me when my transformation
brings me face-to-face with sinfulness.

Surprise me when I am changing
with bright grace and new ways of seeing and knowing you.

And in the midst of all, bring me the gift of new life—
your life.

Amen.

Chapter 3

God Is Present in Our Becoming

The Question: What Am I Becoming?

"Be yourself"; "Be all that you can be"; "Become what you are." These are the familiar phrases of our childhood and, increasingly, of our adult lives. Mature physically and emotionally, find out what you want to do, master the skills to do it, and take your place as a contributing member of society. For most of us, this becomes the goal of our movement from child to adult, and in the process, we leave behind childish things: temper tantrums, the need for instant gratification, and the unlimited choices of our imaginations. The five-year-old dinosaur expert or volcano scientist becomes a lawyer; the princess becomes an aerospace engineer. And yes, occasionally the firefighter becomes a firefighter, because every now and then the gifts and talent needed for the job are made manifest early on in a child's imaginative play.

Somewhere along the line we come to a sometimes disheartening but often freeing realization: we cannot be anything we want to be. I was a senior in college practicing piano some five hours a day when I suddenly realized I was never going to be a great pianist. I had some sorrow about letting go of the unspoken dream, but I had even more freedom when I understood that I did not have to practice five hours a day and could spend my time more wisely and (truth be told) more enjoyably learning to teach well, studying theology, and embracing the gifts I had.

Our parents may have told us, “You can be anything you want to be” with good intention—they did not want to stifle creativity or imagination, and they wanted us to reach for the stars. But that good desire does not take into account the circumstances that surround us as we grow up, nor the gifts, talents, and strengths we have as individuals. It does not help us find what gets us up in the morning or the passion that will ignite our imagination and lead us to the paths we may follow.

Increasingly as well, the path to adulthood is taking longer and longer. For some of us, there are far more choices for education, job, and marriage. Among college-age students, the desire to work for one company for forty years is nearly unthinkable. Marriage is delayed until grad school is finished. Young men and women express a desire to settle down but not to “settle for,” and first jobs and first relationships are unconsciously thought of as “starters.” For others, there are too few choices. Any job is a good job whether it is interesting or not. The luxury of a starter job is often nonexistent. On the other side, the inability to find a job often delays the process of discovering what we are good at and passionate about. Marriage might seem the ultimate logical conclusion of a relationship in which neither partner has had the chance to mature enough to know what they want or need. For many, living together seems to be a viable option that avoids the messiness of commitment.

All this is to say that becoming a professional and an adult in today’s world takes a little longer and seems a little more complex than in previous generations. Regardless of generation or economic circumstance, though, most of us can say we hold in our minds some picture of what adulthood looks like, and it usually has something to do with the commitments we make. Nothing says "adult" to us more than when we have chosen a career, a spouse, or a lifestyle that we believe we will be happy with for years to come. Truthfully, many of us crave at least one, if not all three of those things. We believe somewhere that when we have achieved that, we are finished with our decisions, exploration, and discoveries.

The spiritual life is a slightly different process. In our growing awareness of God, we come to know the permanence of process. This is not a starter relationship nor a beginning job; it is a 24-7 process of discovery. God is a mystery about which there is always more to know. When we stop believing that or stop caring about it, our faith stagnates and becomes irrelevant to our lives. I think that is why so many drop out of the Church for a time as they reach late adolescence and early adulthood. We are confirmed around the age of thirteen, and after that, few (if anyone) encourage us to learn more and differently about God. Our faith and understanding remain stuck at thirteen while everything else we are learning continues to move ahead. How do we make the bridge from a child's faith to an adult faith and from a child's relationship with God to an adult relationship with God? What does "adult" look like in the spiritual life?

I would propose that somewhere along the line, someone decided that being an adult in the spiritual life means that we have "settled down" and made a commitment to someone or something. It means we have no more questions, no more doubts, and that someone has explained it all to us. This could not be further from the truth. To make a commitment to a belief and a particular expression of that belief in a Church, Synagogue, or Mosque is to provide a context in which to ask questions, express doubts, and wrestle with not only our demons but our better angels. It is to believe that we have purpose and meaning beyond what we can see, and it is to commit to the process of seeing it little by little to the end of our lives. It is to believe that someone watches over that process and cares that we make the journey.

Both in our physical and spiritual lives, the fear that "settling down" means "settling for" something can paralyze us so that we make no commitments whatsoever. We ask ourselves, "What if there is someone better out there, a job that is even more fulfilling, or a belief that is even more compelling just around the corner?" A journalism student once interviewed my husband and me regarding a then-recent article that urged women to let go of the idea of an ideal mate and settle for the person she could marry and with whom she could be happy. The student wanted to know what we thought about the article. Both my husband and I were in agreement—marriage is too important to simply "settle for" someone who is nice. The old adage that marriage isn't about who you can live *with* but who you can't live *without* seems true to me, and neither one of us felt we had settled for something less simply to be married.

When I think about the article, though, I realize the author was pointing out our reluctance to make a decision because something better might come along. She wanted people to understand that our fear of losing other options by making a commitment often causes us to overlook some very real possibilities. It is true that making a commitment closes some doors; but making a commitment on any level also sets us on the path of discovering who we are, who God is, and how we make our way with everyone we encounter along the way.

The process of becoming worldly and spiritual adults means recognizing that we will always be "on the road," we will never be 100 percent sure of our steps, and we could be called to plunge headlong into the unknown at any point along the way. The commitments we make to become who we are in our work, our vocation, our relationships, and our belief do not close us off as much as focus our attention on the still, small voice of God, who watches over our becoming and speaks to us through those we encounter, opportunities that come to us, and the gifts and talents he has given to us. If nothing else, our faith tells us that we come from God and we go home to God. All of our commitments are made in the context of that journey. As we grow in mind and body, we also grow in spirit and in the Spirit. Our questions, our doubts, and our strong convictions can and should grow with us, but the basic reality remains the same. God calls us to make the best use of what we have been given in the time we have been given to make our way to him. God invites us to find the best way to express the creative, faithful, and eternal love he first had for us. And though the process of becoming is lifelong (and an occasionally daunting task), we can find our place of rest in the knowledge that we are never alone. God, who knows our possibility, is our constant companion and guide.

The Resting Point:
The Memory That God Is Present in Our Becoming

Meditate and pray through the memory using the following Scripture passages, and recall that God *is present in your becoming.* Take your time and read the Scriptures aloud. Enhance your resting place by letting the meditation carry you into the prayer.

> See what love the Father has bestowed on us that we may be called the children of God. Yet so we are. The reason the world does not know us is that it did not know him. Beloved, we are God's children now; what we shall be has not yet been revealed. We do know that when it is revealed we shall be like him, for we shall see him as he is. Everyone who has this hope based on him makes himself pure, as he is pure.
>
> 1 John 3:2–3

Pause for Meditation

Before we ever wondered who we were and where we were going, someone wondered about us. Our parents could only guess about our personalities and passions. They had only the slightest inkling of how we would change their lives. Theirs was a leap of faith and hope in welcoming us into their family. In the baptism rite, very near the beginning, parents are asked, "Do you clearly understand what you are asking?" I always smile at that question. If we clearly understood everything, we probably wouldn't do it. God keeps us in happy ignorance and allows our future to unfold a day at a time, helping us to roll with the punches, make necessary adjustments, and find out how we are being shaped in the process. To say it is not always easy is an understatement.

But here is the First Letter of John revealing to all who read it with eyes of faith that we are God's children now. Our parents were not the first to care about who we are and how we grow. From the beginning, God cared for every one of us, holding the dream of us in his divine heart. Like parents everywhere, I can imagine God shaking his head every now and then at the surprising, sometimes wonderful, and sometimes troubling things we do. God holds the dream of each of us still and watches over us, and from our first stumbling steps in faith, God shows it to us little by little. "What we shall be has not yet been revealed," John reminds us, and so throughout our lives, we live out what we know and we anticipate what we do not. The clue that we are on the right path is the growing understanding that we are hearing the voice of God getting louder and clearer in every moment and the dawning comprehension that we are, slowly but surely, becoming one with him.

Prayer Action

It might be helpful to reflect and remember what you thought, felt, or dreamed when you were younger as you prepare to pray this Scripture. If you have kept old diaries, journals, or papers from school, reread them to see how you looked at the world. Take those memories into a comfortable space for prayer, and invite God to be present to you. After giving God praise, lift up to God what you once thought, and then reflect on the different ways you think now.

Pray through this passage and come to the first resting point. "What we shall be has not yet been revealed." Give thanks for childhood dreams and thoughts and know that you have changed. Recognize and rejoice that we are still growing in God and in grace. We do not have to know everything now. Simply ask God to show you what you have become thus far, and give thanks for the many things that have already been revealed. Then ask God for the grace to be patient, aware, and open to whatever revelations might be in store for you, remembering that such insights may show up as easily in times of conflict as in times of peace. Resolve to give your whole self as you know it to God's keeping.

Pull the next line of the Scripture into your mind and heart: "When it is revealed we shall be like him, for we shall see him as he is." Only when we are in God will we know ourselves fully, because we will see at last that we are fully known. Pray the line several times, aloud if you like. Then simply rest in it and in the knowledge that God holds the whole of you in love whether you know your next step or not. When you finish your prayer, give thanks for the insights received and return to your daily life, confident in God's presence.

Each year his parents went to Jerusalem for the feast of Passover, and when he was twelve years old, they went up according to festival custom. After they had completed its days, as they were returning, the boy Jesus remained behind in Jerusalem, but his parents did not know it. Thinking that he was in the caravan, they journeyed for a day and looked for him among their relatives and acquaintances, but not finding him, they returned to Jerusalem to look for him. After three days they found him in the temple, sitting in the midst of the teachers, listening to them and asking them questions, and all who heard him were astounded at his understanding and his answers. When his parents saw him, they were astonished, and his mother said to him, "Son, why have you done this to us? Your father and I have been looking for you with great anxiety." And he said to them, "Why were you looking for me? Did you not know that I must be in my Father's house?" But they did not understand what he said to them. He went down with them and came to Nazareth, and was obedient to them; and his mother

> kept all these things in her heart. And Jesus advanced [in] wisdom and age and favor before God and man.
>
> LUKE 2:41–52

Pause for Meditation

I don't think it's mere coincidence that Luke's story of Jesus' coming of age takes place on a journey. Journey is the appropriate metaphor for the discovery moments of our lives. And if Jesus was like us in all things, the need to learn about and articulate the maturing awareness of his unique place in the world would have surely come as he approached his adult life. (In Judaism, the ages of twelve and thirteen remain the traditional time to celebrate the passage into adulthood.) I am always struck that the first thing Mary and Joseph see is their son "listening" and "asking questions." Those two actions provide both a wonderful example and a wise guide for us when we embark on our own path toward self-discovery, self-awareness, and discernment of next steps. Mary and Joseph, who were in a very different place than Jesus, traveled to the Temple and back again, confident in their identity as faithful children of Abraham. They brought their son up so that he would observe Jewish custom and prayer. Jesus saw the need to stay to learn and listen to his own heart and to the wisdom of the elders. His attentiveness and, perhaps, the depth of his questions amazed them. Could someone so young have so much interest in the spiritual life? It seems they asked him questions of their own—maybe his listening challenged them to do the same.

When his parents return, Jesus articulates the need to be "in his Father's house." Jesus understood that God watched over him and was with him in a unique way. It makes sense that he would want to spend time in the Temple, the closest place to God's house that he knew. After he left, it was clear that the grace of God and whatever the elders told him took root, for he continues the process of growing in wisdom and grace.

For Mary and Joseph, this story is, at its core, about losing and finding. They are caught up in the journey and lose track of Jesus. Their only hope is to return to "God's house" and find him. How often in our quest to make the next best move, find ourselves, or get all our questions answered do we lose sight of what grounds us? Jesus stayed and made sure of his ground; Mary and Joseph had to return to find it again and come to a new understanding of themselves as Jesus' parents. The experience stayed with Mary a long time. I have no doubt that when she was tempted to hurry on with things, the memory of the Temple slowed her and made her know more certainly that God watches our becoming with care.

Prayer Action

Read through this gospel story, aloud if possible. Find a comfortable position and relax your body and mind. As much as you are able, open yourself to the quiet. For this moment, however short it is, you do not have anything more pressing than to put yourself in God's presence—in his house. Begin with listening. Imagine yourself next to the boy Jesus and listen, as he does, to every whisper and sigh from God. Bring to mind those who have helped you grow and have revealed God to you. Listen to them. When you are ready, allow any questions you have come to mind. These might be questions about God, faith, life, direction, or even about what is true. Ask those questions slowly, and after each one, listen for any answers or wisdom that God might choose to reveal to you. Know that you will not always get a clear and immediate answer, but God has heard your questions and will answer them in his time and in his way. His grace surrounds you. When you have asked everything you wanted or needed, ask also for the grace to know that God watches over you and gives you what you need. Walk with Jesus and take the presence of God back into your day-to-day life. There grow with him in that same wisdom and grace, resting in the knowledge that God holds what you are becoming in a strong and loving hand.

Prayer for Those Who Wonder What They Are Becoming

God, my creator and my protector,
even now it is not so easy in the growing part of my life
to trust that you are watching over me.

You have said that you know all—
what I have been, what I am, and what I am becoming.

But it is hard to let go of my need to control all of it
and to simply sit and listen for the answers to questions
I didn't know I would be asking.

Help me to listen.

Like those who called themselves children of God,
like Jesus in the Temple, make my heart so still
that your voice becomes the loudest noise within it.

I do not know what I am becoming.

Let my greatest desire be that I become one with you
and my only question, "How can I best do that?"

Amen.

Part II

Remembering God When We Wonder What We Are Going to Do Next

Discovering vocation does not mean scrambling toward some prize just beyond my reach but accepting the treasure of true self I already possess. Vocation does not come from a voice "out there" calling me to be something I am not. It comes from a voice "in here" calling me to be the person I was born to be, to fulfill the original selfhood given me at birth by God.

Parker Palmer, *Let Your Life Speak: Listening for the Voice of Vocation,*

Chapter 4

God Calls Us to Be Who We Are

The Question: What Am I Called to Be?

I will never forget the "aha" expression on Jen's face as we talked about the possibility of doing a service year after she graduated from college. She had been thinking about volunteering for a long time, and this latest conversation had turned to remembering times in her childhood and youth when she might have been drawn to helping others. With delight she recalled that she had wanted to be a princess in her late childhood, around the age when many girls wonder what that might be like. But it wasn't pretty dresses and jeweled crowns that captured her imagination. "I didn't really think about those things," she said, "though I'm sure they caught my eye. Instead, I was thinking that if I were a princess, then people would cook and clean for me and I would have time to help others." The impetus to help others was already there, filtered through a child's imagination and the practical problem-solving only children can do. A person needs time to help others, and if she were a princess, then the normal needs of cooking and cleaning would be taken care of by someone else and she could devote that time to her desire to serve.

Jen ultimately decided not to volunteer full time, but her desire for and call to service did not go away. She spent a year advising other students, and then decided to go back to school to learn this advising skill even better. Along the way, she continued to volunteer in many of the opportunities that came her way—from tutoring school children to visiting juveniles in jail. Each experience showed her different possibilities for using her skills in math and science, her passion for teaching and advising, and her long-term aspirations to help others. I love the idea that what had been present in Jen's childhood showed up in college where she honed natural talents for the sciences. I am confident that no matter what she does next, those gifts will continue to manifest themselves in new and varied ways.

"What am I called to be?" "Why did God make me?" In the catechism of my childhood, the answer was short and succinct: "To know, love, and serve God in this world and be happy with God in the next." I was quite a bit older when I understood the full import of this statement. Knowing, loving, and serving God is the rich soil of our livelihood regardless of what we do. When the impulse to choose or change our direction comes into our hearts, it is God's invitation to see if we might order our gifts differently so that we might know God a little better, love God a little more, and serve God with our whole being. Sometimes all that takes is a commitment to continue what we are already doing with renewed dedication, thanksgiving, and hope. Sometimes we have to refocus our aim, leaving hometown, jobs, schools, and sometimes friends to find out what God has in store for us.

In my own life I have dealt with the question of "what to do next" in the usual transition periods around graduation and job-hunting and in family decisions as we dealt with aging parents and potential moves. There were also the unusual moments when jobs did not work out or sudden interruptions in our lives forced us to look in a new direction. I am now at the age when I can reflect on my experiences and impart the wisdom we all learn sooner or later: "The question of what to do next doesn't go away just because you have made this one decision." I can say this much, though: God does not call us to be something we are not; nor does God ask us to hide our best selves. We toil in classrooms, garages, homes, stores, and offices. In each place the insistent love of God pushes us to live fully into our lives as disciples and believers.

So why can't we be settled once and for all? We move in different directions for many reasons. Sometimes it is our choice when we realize that what we are doing no longer expresses the best of who we are or the people with whom we work no longer bring out the best in us. Sometimes change is forced on us when we lose a job. Occasionally, outside pressures compel us to stay in one place when we would rather be doing something else. At the heart of the matter is this: We need to do something to make our living—put food on the table, a roof over our heads, and support our families. God willing, it is something we enjoy doing. But that is not the sum total of our lives. God also exhorts us to make this living worthwhile. If we are very lucky, what we do to support ourselves and our families will also be the vocation by which we build up the people of God. It may also be the case that our vocation is not the same as our paid employment; rather, it may look like volunteer time in an afterschool program, at a tutoring center, or in a nursing home. There, the same gifts we have glimpsed all our lives can be refocused and used for the sake of the kingdom of God. God challenges us to share what we have been and also what we have become in the world to build up the community of faith and to help the world make its way home to God.

God rejoices and calls out to us to be who we are for him and in loving service to others. The great relief in this knowledge is that we already possess everything we need—God's gifts to us at our conception. So many people have told me that they discovered what they were really good at through an internship or volunteer experience they thought was relatively inconsequential. One woman, a theater major, found herself in fundraising and discovered she was really good at it—not only because she had learned how to improvise and speak to people but also because she had lived much of the time with her grandmother and had learned how to talk to and care for adults much older than she was. Her gifts of compassion, an outgoing nature, and a can-do attitude led her to the world of nonprofit fundraising, where she continues to hone her understanding of stewardship and encourages people to support what they love.

Where there is great relief, however, there is also great challenge. What if being who we are means we must change what we do or the way we do it? The risk of being a disciple is not that we might change the world; it's that we open ourselves to being changed in the process. Once we name God as the most important being in our lives and order our lives around him, we cannot help but conform our lives to his will. It is not always going to be convenient, easy, or effortless. Our understanding of that, as often as not, makes us hesitant and unsure. "Am I doing the right thing?" For those of us who get caught up in the anxiety of the question, the memory that God calls us to be who we are (and helps us find out who that is) can be a great comfort indeed.

Resting Point: The Memory That God Calls Us to Be Who We Are

Meditate and pray through the memory using the following Scripture passages, and recall that God calls *you to come as you are.* Take your time and read the Scriptures aloud. Enhance your resting place by letting the meditation carry you into the prayer.

As [Jesus] was walking by the Sea of Galilee, he saw two brothers, Simon who is called Peter, and his brother Andrew, casting a net into the sea; they were fishermen. He said to them, "Come after me, and I will make you fishers of men." At once they left their nets and followed him. He walked along from there and saw two other brothers, James, the son of Zebedee, and his brother John. They were in a boat, with their father Zebedee, mending their nets. He called them, and immediately they left their boat and their father and followed him.

MATTHEW 4:18–22

Pause for Meditation

I have always wondered how these fishermen felt when Jesus appears out of nowhere and says, "Come after me." Fishing was what they were good at; it was how they made their living and cared for their families. Fishing gave them a place and an identity in the world. Jesus must have sensed this, for he appeals to them at the very heart of their self-understanding: "I will make you fishers of men." Everything they had learned on the job—the patience, the persistence, the way to read the ripples that indicated a school of fish beneath the surface, the secret knowledge of where fish go when it's hot or when it's cool—all of these gifts and talents could and would be of use in a new endeavor. Jesus did not call them to become rocket scientists or magistrates. He called them to come into the fullness of who they were, to imagine what that might look like in a different set of circumstances, and to use their gifts for God's sake and the sake of others. Today, we encourage people to take their time, pray, and consult with trusted friends or mentors. The very suddenness with which these fishermen respond is the stuff of legend and may seem, in turn, inspirational or foolhardy to us. But Jesus' call into the fullness of identity goes out to us as well. And whether we respond quickly or slowly to that call, Jesus promises that he will always lead the way and will not try to make us into something other than who we are.

Prayer Action

I invite you to enter this story in a particular way—by literally placing yourself in the midst of it. First, quiet yourself and find a comfortable place to write. Read the passage from Matthew aloud, and ask Jesus to show you the graces of this passage in your life. Think about all the places in which Jesus might appear to you; then, when you're ready, fill in the blanks below, using the guide that follows the passage.

As [Jesus] was walking by the ______1______, he saw ______2______, ______3______ who is called ______4______, who was ______5______; s/he was a ______6______. He said "Come after me, and I will make you ______7______." At once s/he left his/her ______8______ and followed him.

1. The place you do the bulk of your work (paid or not)
2. How you identify yourself (woman, man, student, son, daughter, and so forth)
3. Your formal name
4. Your nickname, if you have one
5. Something you do on a daily basis in your work
6. What you do or study (chemical engineer, musician, housewife or husband, mechanic, businessperson, and so forth)

7. Whatever you said in number 6, repeat and add the words *for the kingdom of God*
8. Whatever you use in your daily work or study

Now reread this passage with your answers and reflect on what it would mean to be a musician or a mechanic (or whatever else you named) for the kingdom of God. What gifts, skills, and talents would be used again? How in your daily life can you refocus those gifts to make this call of Jesus concrete? Finish your prayer by thanking God for any insights you have gained and for the grace of believing that God knows who you are and calls you to be only and fully that.

Then Samuel asked Jesse, "Are these all the sons you have?" Jesse replied, "There is still the youngest, but he is tending the sheep." Samuel said to Jesse, "Send for him; we will not sit down to eat until he arrives here." Jesse had the young man brought to them. He was ruddy, a youth with beautiful eyes, and good looking. The LORD said: There—anoint him, for this is the one! Then Samuel, with the horn of oil in hand, anointed him in the midst of his brothers, and from that day on, the spirit of the LORD rushed upon David. Then Samuel set out for Ramah.

1 SAMUEL 16:11–13

Pause for Meditation

In all of Scripture, the story of the shepherd boy who was anointed a king stands out as one of the more unlikely scenarios. Surely there were more sophisticated and experienced people who could be king. But true to form, God called a shepherd to be the shepherd of Israel. Samuel's words speak to all of us of the importance of answering the call to be more of who we are. "We will not sit down," Samuel says, until he arrives here." In the same way, the Church needs every person to be fully who they are and alive in their knowledge of the love of God.

Hundreds of years after David was anointed king of Israel, the great prophet Ezekiel confirms what the story of David tells us: a shepherd was precisely what God had in mind to symbolize his care for the people of Israel. The shepherd feeds the sheep, gathers the lost, cares for the sick, and carries the lambs. So powerful was the image that Jesus used it to describe himself. In David, God chose a shepherd to be a shepherd in a way he never dreamed of being. The gifts that made David a good shepherd were precisely those that would make him able to be a good king, despite his very human sinfulness.

This is how God calls us—out of what we do well into what we will do best. When we see ourselves as workers in the kingdom and servants of the Lord, we find fullness in everything we do—no matter how small it may seem. We will not all be kings; we will not all have songs sung about us or books written, but we will have the grace of God to transform our lives and allow us to use everything we have been given. Rest there, and the next steps may be easier to find.

Prayer Action

Bring the passage from 1 Samuel to your workspace or to the place where you spend the most time. Find five minutes during the day to read the Scripture aloud, then quiet your heart and ask God to come to you with an understanding of who you are now. Listen as that understanding unfolds and rejoice in it. Are you a grocery checker? Rejoice in that. Are you a student? Give thanks for that. Are you a masseuse? Invite God to help you be grateful for what you are learning in that role.

Very gently ask God to reveal the fullness of who you are in this work or occupation—the gifts you bring to it, the skills you have learned from it, and the talent you may have for it. Gently invite God to show you both how you serve him now and other ways you might serve him with your gifts.

When you are finished reflecting, find a posture that opens you up; lift your head, open your hands, and offer yourself to God for the work God might have you do. Rejoice again in the many ways your gifts can be used for building up the people of God. When you are finished, rest for a moment and return to your day.

Prayer for Those Who Wonder What They Are Called to Be

Lord, God of all, who is in all and through all,
I wonder who I am and what I do best, even now.

I am comfortable in the familiarity
of my work or school or home,
but truthfully, I am a little anxious
about what might lie ahead.

So, Lord, I ask for the grace you gave David
who saw that being a shepherd could be a way of being
the image of God.

I ask for the grace of Peter and Andrew
who were called to be exactly who they were
for your sake and the sake of the world.

I ask for the grace you gave to Mary Magdalene
who served you as disciple,
all the while silently listening to your words
until you called her to proclaim those words to the world
so that others might be your disciples too.

Whatever it is that you have made me,
whatever gifts you have given me,
let me use them where I am with joy and gladness
and let me give them back to you so that you can show me
how you want me to use them tomorrow.

Help me rest in the sure knowledge
that you will use them as you see fit.

Amen.

Chapter 5

What You Have Is Enough to Share

The Question: What Do I Have to Give?

The intellectual gifts and talents of the students I know constantly amaze me. One talks with ease about electromagnetic currents; another is a wonderful French horn player; still another speaks with passion about the veterinarian she hopes to be someday. The students are a little more puzzled when I ask them to name some of their other gifts and how they might use them in their chosen field of study. "What do your friends or family say you are good at? How would they describe you?"

The students often meet these questions with silent consideration. Sometimes they are genuinely stumped. Others have told me it sounds like bragging if they point out their good characteristics. Still others have always identified themselves as "being good at math," and the culture encourages everyone to find the skill or talent that will make them "productive." Being the best often means being the smartest, the most talented, or the most competitive. Traits like listening well become secondary and the ability to see the complexities of a situation is lost in the midst of instant-messaging and sound bites. We forget sometimes that these human traits are just as valuable to the world as the facts we learn.

The issue becomes more acute when a student is considering switching majors or someone is trying to decide on a different career path. "What gifts do you bring to a new endeavor? What have you already displayed in your current field? What are you good at?" becomes "Am I good enough for anything?" or "How can I even think about changing majors or jobs?" The trajectory of our education and experience pushes us to think about getting better at what we do. No doubt this is important, but what happens when "what we do" is no longer viable? We lose our job or we discover that our real passion lies elsewhere or, in a twist of fate, the skill or talent we relied on is lost to us. I wonder if along with getting good at what we do, we might spend more time getting good at *who we are*. The characteristics of love, compassion, organization, concern, teaching, listening, connecting, and so on are traits that will last a lifetime, regardless of the jobs we hold. "But what if it isn't enough?" we say. And underlying that, "What if my gifts are dismissed, unwelcome, or unappreciated?"

Into this new set of questions and worries comes a wonderful story of feeding a lot of people with just a little. I first heard this interpretation of feeding the 5,000 from singer-songwriter John McCutcheon, who pointed out one of the true insights of the miracle. In John's version, a child gives up the small amount of food he has—five loaves and two fish—in innocent belief that the crowd's hunger can be sated with this meager amount.

What was the real miracle in this story? Tradition tells us it is the multiplication of the loaves and fish, an indication that the word and presence of God is more than enough to fill us all. A priest friend of mine suggested it was the baskets—where did they get twelve baskets in which to put the leftovers? John McCutcheon thoughtfully talks about the child and wonders what family or community raised this child to believe that what he or she had was enough to share and everyone would be satisfied.

As a faith community, we believe God gave us our gifts and talents to serve the whole. God blessed them and broke them and invited us to share them with the world for the sake of the reign of God. The vast majority of us suffer at one time or another with questions about what we have to offer anyone and whether our gifts will be enough for the challenges that lie ahead. When we have to make decisions about our future, those doubts suddenly move into high gear, sometimes threatening to overwhelm us altogether. *What if I get it wrong? What if I hate this in about two years? What if this is not what I'm meant to be doing?*

For all of us who have found ourselves questioning and doubting the next move, McCutcheon's insight is our resting point. What we have been given is enough to share, and everyone will be satisfied. We say this with the utter conviction that we are God's children. In the hidden and not-so-hidden places of our lives, some of us have the grace of listening or the graces of leading or organizing, praying or preaching, teaching, serving, or loving others. We get better at being God's children when we bring forward our little individual gifts and give them in love, trusting that God will make of them as much as is needed and that all of them will build up the community of faith. The gifts we have been given cannot be depleted, and the more we bring them forth, the greater confidence we will have that they will be with us no matter what we do next.

The Resting Point: The Memory That God Has Given Us Enough to Share

Meditate and pray through the memory using the following Scripture passages, and recall that God has *gifted you and desires you to use these gifts for others.* Take your time and read the Scriptures aloud. Enhance your resting place by letting the meditation carry you into the prayer.

> After this, Jesus went across the Sea of Galilee [of Tiberias]. A large crowd followed him, because they saw the signs he was performing on the sick. Jesus went up on the mountain, and there he sat down with his disciples. The Jewish feast of Passover was near. When Jesus raised his eyes and saw that a large crowd was coming to him, he said to Philip, "Where can we buy enough food for them to eat?" He said this to test him, because he himself knew what he was going to do. Philip answered him, "Two hundred days' wages worth of food would not be enough for each of them to have a little [bit]." One of his disciples, Andrew, the brother of Simon Peter, said to him, "There is a boy here who has five barley loaves and two fish; but what good are these for so many?" Jesus said, "Have the people recline." Now there was a great deal of grass in that place. So the men reclined, about five thousand in number. Then Jesus took the loaves, gave thanks, and distributed them to those who were reclining, and also as much of the fish as they wanted. When they had had their fill, he said to his disciples, "Gather the fragments left over, so that nothing will be wasted." So they collected them, and filled twelve wicker baskets with fragments from the five barley loaves that had been more than they could eat. When the people saw the sign he had done, they said, "This is truly the Prophet, the one who is to come into the world."
>
> John 6:1–14

Pause for Meditation

All the gospels recount this miraculous feeding story. John's version is the only one in which a child plays an active part, making it a favorite for religion teachers who want to inspire their young charges. The barley loaves and fish presented by the child were the food found among the poor. It is amazing to think that so many people were so hungry to hear what Jesus had to say that they did not think about what they would eat later in the day, or perhaps they were so used to not eating that they just accepted it as part of their lives. In any case, the child willingly gave over what he had, however meager it seemed. While this is certainly a tale of the abundance of Christ and our hunger for the life he brings, it is also a tale of confidence in the face of utter foolishness and believing that we can always feed just one more. This is the starting point for our resting place: remembering that God can take what we have, however little it may seem to us or to others, and with grace, make it more than enough so that we might share what we have with the whole world.

Prayer Action

Find a comfortable place in which to rest attentively and read the story of this miracle, paying careful attention to the need of the people and the doubt of the disciples. When you are ready, call to mind the needs of the people in your family, church, neighborhood, and world. Who is in need of love, peace, comfort, or challenge? Lift those people up to God, and hold them in your heart for a few minutes.

Reflect on the gifts you have been given as a child of God. What do you have to share with any of those you are holding in your heart? Make a list of these gifts, no matter how inconsequential they may seem, and include everything you can think of. Now imagine yourself approaching the Lord with your gifts and offering them with a child's confidence that it will be enough to share. Imagine Jesus taking your gifts and giving thanks for them. Imagine him blessing your gifts and asking you to distribute them as far as they will go. Feel the weight of your gifts and experience the joy that you can give them to anyone you meet.

Proclaim your thanks to God for this moment of recognition, and ask for the grace to begin to share your gifts with all those you meet.

> So the word of the LORD came to [Elijah]: Arise, go to Zarephath of Sidon and stay there. I have commanded a widow there to feed you. He arose and went to Zarephath. When he arrived at the entrance of the city, a widow was there gathering sticks; he called out to her, "Please bring me a small cupful of water to drink." She left to get it, and he called out after her, "Please bring along a crust of bread." She said, "As the LORD, your God, lives, I have nothing baked; there is only a handful of flour in my jar and a little oil in my jug. Just now I was collecting a few sticks, to go in and prepare something for myself and my son; when we have eaten it, we shall die." Elijah said to her, "Do not be afraid. Go and do as you have said. But first make me a little cake and bring it to me. Afterwards you can prepare something for yourself and your son. For the LORD, the God of Israel, says: The jar of flour shall not go empty, nor the jug of oil run dry, until the day when the LORD sends rain upon the earth." She left and did as Elijah had said. She had enough to eat for a long time—he and she and her household. The

> jar of flour did not go empty, nor the jug of oil run dry, according to the word of the LORD spoken through Elijah.
>
> 1 KINGS 17:8–16

Pause for Meditation

The drought that comes upon the land of Sidon leaves everyone with a little less than they had before. The widow whom Elijah visits has eked out an existence for herself and her son and is prepared to use the last bit of flour and oil she has before both of them will die. These are not the ingredients of luxury; they are the stuff of survival. At Elijah's insistence, the woman gives the little she has and discovers it is enough. With God's grace, Elijah, the woman, her son, and everyone else who was in that house carried on through the drought and then lived on in the story and memory of Israel.

Reflected in this woman, I see the faces of countless men and women of the world who have given over their last crust to feed someone who was starving—often children or the elderly. I see parents who have gone without luxuries and even necessities to give their children better than they had themselves. It does not always turn out as well as it did for the woman who fed Elijah. I recall one homeless family who was living in a tent and whose story was told in the local newspaper. My daughter was young at the time and we were counting pennies, but we had a roof over our heads and food on the table, so I was moved to buy some food items and find the place where they were staying. I remember approaching the tent; the couple was gracious, but their young son—a little older than my daughter—offered her a slice of cheese. They needed many things but were not afraid to share what they had with someone else—even though we had more. I was humbled that day and learned a little more about sharing. Since then, I have wondered what would happen if everyone were that generous, not just with food, but with their lives.

I like that Elijah tells her, "Do not be afraid." Sometimes, thinking we don't have anything to share keeps us from moving in new directions, trying new things, and changing our habits. God has given us the gifts we need to share with the world. God has also given others gifts to share with us. Together, we can discover new joy in what we have been doing and in what we might do in the future.

Prayer Action

If possible, find a comfortable place in your kitchen to read through the aforementioned passage. Put flour and oil on the table, and invite God to be present to you. As you quiet yourself, imagine making bread every day for you and your family or friends until the flour and oil are almost gone.

Now imagine one more person coming in to be fed and wondering how you can possibly do it. Place that anxiety in the hand of the Lord as you ponder your next steps, and ask yourself, "What is in short supply for me today? Is it my love, patience, compassion, sense of justice, or sense of humor? What would happen if I just begin to use them as if they would last forever?" Lay whatever is in short supply on the table beside the flour and oil. If you are not in the kitchen, hold them in your heart before you and thank God for what you have.

Keep your attention on the gifts God has already given you, and when you are ready, ask God for the grace to share them unconditionally, trusting that God will provide enough to give to anyone who asks and even to those who do not.

Prayer for Those Who Wonder What They Have to Give

O Lord, who came that we might have life
and have it abundantly,
whose mercy and compassion pour out over the whole earth
and who gives us what we need in due season,
you have given us gifts of the Spirit to build your Church,
you have given us talents and abilities
to find our place in this world.

May the first of these always inform and shape the second.

May our love be the guide for our life's work;
our compassion, the fine edge of our vocation.

Most of all, help us to know that food comes
in all kinds of disguises,
and however little we think we have been given,
it is enough to share with the whole world.

Help us to understand
that when we share what we have with our whole being
and out of love for you and one another,
everyone will be satisfied.

Amen.

Chapter 6

Nothing Is Lost

The Question: Have I Wasted My Time?

Roy, a seminarian, was spending a little time in the university Newman Center, working with students and doing occasional presentations. In the first few weeks he was at the Center, we had the usual conversations about school and majors and what he liked about the seminary. He told me he had been a civil engineer out of school and wondered aloud how that was going to help him in his priesthood. We laughed about the number of priests we knew who also doubled as the part-time maintenance guy at their parish and thought that such a knowledge base just might come in handy. Toward the end of our conversation, there was a pause and we said, nearly simultaneously, "How would it be to build the city of God?"

I have thought about that conversation in the years since. Roy wondered if the time spent learning civil engineering had been wasted. But throughout Scripture, God has found a way to use the unique gifts and talents of those whom he calls. Abraham, a man who knew what it was to be settled in one place, was called to settle in another. With God's strange prompting, a woman, whose local reputation suggested that men could find comfort and pleasure in her company, welcomed two strangers and offered them safety and security. A zealous defender of the Law of Israel became an even more zealous defender of the Christian faith.

As a civil engineer, Roy looked forward to building bridges, roads, airstrips, and buildings. When he entered the seminary, that gift was not exchanged or lost; rather, it was redirected and refocused. As a priest, he might not build an actual building (though more and more priests get that experience), but his gifts could be used to build up the community of faith. Even Saint Paul compares an apostle's work to that of a "master builder" (1 Corinthians 3:10), who builds on the foundation already laid by Jesus Christ. I have no doubt that this is one of Roy's favorite passages.

I find it amazing that God does not waste a precious minute of our lives. God's voice speaks to us in imaginative play, through friends and confidantes, in works of fiction, and in books of Scripture. God reaches out to talk to us through our thoughts, dreams, and daily work. In truth, God never stops trying to get our attention. If we take the time to reflect on the many places in which God might have revealed something of his will for our lives, we might all be surprised at the way we have been guided even when we knew nothing about it.

A great deal of our realization of God's presence, though, comes in hindsight. I trace the turning of my life and I can see that from early on I was drawn to teaching, and I can see that I have taught in nearly every situation in which I found myself. It hasn't always been in classrooms, but that is where I started because I did not see how I could teach anywhere else. Along the way, God revealed other gifts that have been a part of my vocation, and God has surprised me with different ways in which those could be used. I know too that I sometimes assailed God with questions about the next step to take. But God rarely communicates in handwriting on the wall and dramatic dreams—much to our dismay. Our task is to remember what God has said and done in our lives to this moment and find in that the path of our unfolding. The writers of the Wisdom literature knew this. They drew the wisdom of the proverbs, the beauty of the psalms, and the contemplation of life and God from their experiences of living. For the Wisdom writers, God is always an unseen presence, and what we know, we have learned from the works of his hand and from his words as others heard them.

What we know is this: nothing is ever lost or wasted. There is no state in life, no major in school, no job we have in or through which God cannot reveal the gifts he has given us or the way in which he wants us to go. If I have a gift for teaching, then I will teach whether that is in a classroom, a meeting, or a conversation. If one of my gifts is compassionate listening, I may well become a safe haven for others in whatever work I find myself. Our skills and talents may well turn us toward particular areas of work, but it is our gifts and passions that guide how we make that work meaningful for ourselves and those around us.

Every twist and turn in the road is another perspective in which to see. Every interruption is an invitation to go a little deeper, look a little more intently, or listen a little harder to what God is saying to us. Every experience is shaped by what has come before, and we discover a little more of who we are and what we have to give in every single one. When the work is not what we want to do, our challenge is to see which of our gifts have been brought out in that particular job. Which have been strengthened and shaped? Have others emerged? In positive experiences, we might ask what is bringing peace, joy, and satisfaction in what we are doing and how might we continue on the path. Our vocation, which is another way of talking about where our gifts are harnessed by God's call, is discovered and formed in prayer and in practice. And even our bad choices can help us to hone our gifts for the next step along the way. Nothing is wasted.

When we remember that God is present in every situation and talks to us through each encounter, we are freed from thinking that we must have one job over another or move in this direction rather than that one. We can rest in the knowledge that our gifts will be made manifest, that none will be lost, and that God will make the most of any decision we choose. Then we can take the next best step as we see it and look down the path for more.

The Resting Point: The Memory That Nothing Is Lost in God

Meditate and pray through the memory using the following Scripture passages, and recall that God *does not waste our moments or our giftedness.* Take your time and read the Scriptures aloud. Enhance your resting place by letting the meditation carry you into the prayer.

> Now Saul, still breathing murderous threats against the disciples of the Lord, went to the high priest and asked him for letters to the synagogues in Damascus, that, if he should find any men or women who belonged to the Way, he might bring them back to Jerusalem in chains. On his journey, as he was nearing Damascus, a light from the sky suddenly flashed around him. He fell to the ground and heard a voice saying to him, "Saul, Saul, why are you persecuting me?" He said, "Who are you, sir?" The reply came, "I am Jesus, whom you are persecuting. Now get up and go into the city and you will be told what you must do." The men who were traveling with him stood speechless, for they heard the voice but could see no one. Saul got up from the ground, but when he opened his eyes he could

see nothing; so they led him by the hand and brought him to Damascus. For three days he was unable to see, and he neither ate nor drank.

There was a disciple in Damascus named Ananias, and the Lord said to him in a vision, "Ananias." He answered, "Here I am, Lord." The Lord said to him, "Get up and go to the street called Straight and ask at the house of Judas for a man from Tarsus named Saul. He is there praying, and [in a vision] he has seen a man named Ananias come in and lay [his] hands on him, that he may regain his sight." But Ananias replied, "Lord, I have heard from many sources about this man, what evil things he has done to your holy ones in Jerusalem. And here he has authority from the chief priests to imprison all who call upon your name." But the Lord said to him, "Go, for this man is a chosen instrument of mine to carry my name before Gentiles, kings, and Israelites, and I will show him what he will have to suffer for my name." So Ananias went and entered the house; laying his hands on him, he said, "Saul, my brother, the Lord has sent me, Jesus who appeared to you on the way by which you came, that you may regain your sight and be filled with the holy Spirit." Immediately things like scales fell from his eyes and he regained his sight. He got up and was baptized, and when he had eaten, he recovered his strength. He stayed some days with the disciples in Damascus, and he began at once to proclaim Jesus in the synagogues, that he is the Son of God.

ACTS 9:1–20

Pause for Meditation

This is really the tale of two people whose gifts in one part of their lives were pressed into service in another. We know Saul (named Paul in a different version of this story). His life was spent upholding the Jewish Law with passion and dedication, even to the point of imprisoning and killing Christians. A vision of the risen Christ knocked him to the ground and set him on a different path. Perhaps he wondered what he had been doing all this time. Were the young-adult years of his life wasted? Jesus did not answer that for him, but gave him an opportunity to refocus his passion and zeal. After his baptism, Saul used his gifts of rhetoric and persuasion and his fervor for the truth to build up the Church.

In the second half of the story, Ananias had to draw on his own gifts of healing, hospitality, compassion, and faith in God to care for a man he considered an enemy. Ananias was skeptical about treating Saul, but his gifts could not be wasted. The Lord's message to him was to see Saul as a brother in Christ and not to hide in his own community.

Paul's gifts were refocused; Ananias' gifts were put to use in a different context. God does not put boundaries around our gifts, but exhorts us to see the varied ways in which we might use them, knowing that they have been shaped, strengthened, and honed by every experience that has come before.

Prayer Action

At first glance it may seem odd to pray with a story of radical conversion. We will rarely be knocked to the ground by a vision or struck blind for three days until we figure out we are not in charge. But we may find ourselves suddenly changing direction and wondering what we've been doing the whole time. We might find ourselves offering the gift of compassion to someone we have considered an enemy. We will be suspicious, distrustful, and cautious, and still God will prod us and poke us to see that our gifts can be used in ways we could not have imagined. Sometimes we are brought to that lesson kicking, screaming, and blind as a bat because that is the only way God could get our attention. The only thing we can do, then, is to trust that our past experiences have prepared us in some way for what is happening now, that nothing has been wasted, and that God guides the process even if the whole map is not laid out for us.

Begin your prayer by finding a quiet place and simply sitting with the intention of opening your heart to God. If it's helpful, have paper and pencil nearby to keep track of your thoughts. Begin by breathing in and out, relaxing your shoulders and hands (places where we often carry our worry), and simply reflecting on where you are and what you have been doing in your life to this point. Allow yourself the time and space to answer the following questions. Do not force the answers. If it's helpful, write them down: (1) What gives me joy or engages me? (2) What am I good at and where do I spend my energy? (3) Where, in my current situation, do these joys or gifts come out? (4) What gifts and joys will stay with me regardless of where I go from here?

Remaining in an attentive prayer posture, read the passage aloud, pausing if something strikes you. Imagine yourself with Saul, blind and waiting for three days to see what he would do next. Use the time to remember your answers to the previous questions. Your gifts have been part of you from the beginning. Nothing has been lost or wasted. Perhaps they just need to be brought out or, like Saul, you will find yourself using them for a new chapter in your life.

Turn your attention to Ananias, whose gifts were now focused on an enemy rather than on his community. This may have been his first challenge: to be an instrument of God's love to someone who would just as soon have killed him as look at him. But Christian love, compassion, and healing were his gifts. How could he refuse to use them? How can you? The gift is not lost simply because we may have trouble using it. Continue to breathe gently and open yourself to God's voice telling you to trust that what you have learned, the way you have been shaped, and the gifts you have been given will still be a part of you wherever you are. Thank God for the insights and gently return to what is next for you.

> I have seen the business that God has given to mortals to be busied about. God has made everything appropriate to its time, but has put the timeless into their hearts so they cannot find out, from beginning to end, the work which God has done. I recognized that there is nothing better than to rejoice and to do well during life. Moreover, that all can eat and drink and enjoy the good of all their toil—this is a gift of God. I recognized that whatever God does will endure forever; there is no adding to it, or taking from it. Thus has God done that he may be revered. What now is has already been; what is to be, already is: God retrieves what has gone by.
>
> Ecclesiastes 3:10–15

Pause for Meditation

Ecclesiastes, like all of Wisdom literature, draws on life experience to tell us about God and the nature of the human spirit. Here we overhear the author reflect that the work we do is appropriate at every moment and that we can enjoy the good of our toil. It is a gift of God. If we read between the lines, we can hear him tell us that nothing is wasted. Good can be found throughout our lives. That is easy to hear when we have clear evidence of the ways in which our gifts are used. But what happens when we realize that the job, the major, or the life situation does not bring out the best in us? Even then, what God has given us endures and God can retrieve whatever we think we have lost. Nothing we have done need be wasted effort. God restores and brings our gifts to the next place we find ourselves.

Prayer Action

Prepare yourself to pray this passage by finding a space to sit quietly in a position of attentive rest. Have a pencil and paper nearby in case you want to keep notes to guide your prayer. Invite God to be present to you and, when you are ready, gently read through the passage. Pause to reflect on: (1) What has God given you to be busied about? (2) What have you learned of God and yourself from these works? (3) Where have you done well and feel as if you have contributed something?

Rest in the comfort that all those things are held in God in trust and that God will give them to you as you need and ask for them as you trod forward on the path that lies ahead. God holds you in love and rejects nothing of what is true, beautiful, and loving in your life. Thank God for your insights and gently return to your life.

Prayer for Those Who Wonder If They Have Wasted Their Time

Good and gracious God,
you who hold our time in your hands
and count every minute of life as precious,
watch over me now.

I am not always sure I am in the right place
nor am I always confident that I am doing the right thing.

I sometimes think there is a better way
to use what you have given me
and a better place to feel that I am of use and precious to you.

Help me see that in every time
I am being shaped by your love
and the work you have given me to do.

Help me to know in my heart that I might need to be here
before I can be wherever "there" is.

But most of all, dear God,
give me the grace to use what you have given me
in every place you take me
so that when I come to the next,
whether you led me there or I followed,
I may be found ready for your service
and richer in grace than when I started.

Amen.

Chapter 7

God's Path Is the Answer

The Question: Where Am I Going?

My decision to resign from my seminary teaching position "to see what else was out there" began as a nearly imperceptible nudge from God that gradually developed into a sensation of being pushed by an unstoppable force. For that two-year period, I spent long hours in prayer, asking for a sign that this was the right thing to do and for the direction in which I was to move. I thought it might be ministry, but I wasn't sure what kind of ministry, and the fact that I had experienced a similar sensation when I left ministry to pursue further education and a teaching position did not help. I didn't understand why God would call me from ministry to teaching only to call me back again. We did a lot of sparring back in those days.

Finally, and somewhat blindly, I made the decision to resign but had not yet written the formal letter to my dean nor really spoken to anyone. It was late spring, and I decided to make the resignation effective in June of the following year to give the school time to find a replacement and me to find a job. The custom at the time was for the graduating class to present a special award to the faculty or staff member who, in their opinion, contributed the most theologically, spiritually, and communally to the school. The vote was done in secret and had to be unanimous or it was not awarded. That year I was surprised when my name was called—shocked into wordlessness actually. When the awards banquet was over, I crossed the street to the chapel at the Catholic Center, went up to the altar, laid down the cross I had been given, and said to God, "You're not going to make this easy, are you?"

When I wrote my letter to the seminary community telling them of my decision, I said, "Sometimes when we ask God a question, he gives us a path instead of an answer." After years of teaching, my path was curving in a different direction, stretching beyond where I could see. I resigned without knowing what was coming next, just that I had to go and see what God had in store for me. I was blessed to have landed in a place where I have seen and experienced grace in many ways through the students and adults with whom I minister. I also feel certain that my years of teaching and forming men and women for ministry prepared me for this service in ways I am still discovering.

I don't know what the next step is because the path winds ever before me around the corner and out of sight. What I am doing now is, in some way, honing my skills for whatever is next. I am convinced that God holds us in our walking and, when we are most ready (in his divine wisdom and not in ours), he reveals another section of our path. The path is God's answer to our periodic questions. It is neither definitive for us nor entirely satisfactory. Sometimes it is downright frustrating. And still, God invites us to enjoy the trip while we are walking—making our way ever closer to him.

The Resting Point: The Memory That God's Path Is the Answer

Meditate and pray through the memory using the following Scripture passages, and recall that God *answers by leading us on our path.* Take your time and read the Scriptures aloud. Enhance your resting place by letting the meditation carry you into the prayer.

Keep me safe, O God;
 in you I take refuge.
I say to the LORD,
 you are my Lord,
 you are my only good.
As for the holy ones who are in the land,
 they are noble,
 in whom is all my delight.
They multiply their sorrows
 who court other gods....
LORD, my allotted portion and my cup,
 you have made my destiny secure.
Pleasant places were measured out for me;
 fair to me indeed is my inheritance.

I bless the LORD who counsels me;
 even at night my heart exhorts me.
I keep the LORD always before me;
 with him at my right hand, I shall never be shaken.
Therefore my heart is glad, my soul rejoices;
 my body also dwells secure,
For you will not abandon my soul to Sheol,
 nor let your devout one see the pit.

You will show me the path to life,
abounding joy in your presence,
the delights at your right hand forever.

PSALM 16

Pause for Meditation

I love the psalms. They lay every human emotion and experience before the Lord and express the confidence that God will hear the prayer and change the one who prays for good. The psalmist has the faith that God even now is intervening in his or her life and that, in time, all things will be ordered toward God. Psalm 16 expresses the centrality of God for the psalmist. There is no other one who commands attention and no other god to whom the psalmist will turn for refuge and safety. "You will show me the path to life," sings the psalmist. We would expect no less from a God who has chosen his people in love.

But look at the other things God does in this psalm. God makes the destiny secure. He counsels, he shows. In short, God holds our future until we step into it. He does not force, as God's love is not competitive. Rather, he invites, challenges, and calls us to be wholly who we are as a child of God, made in the image of the Creator.

So many other things in our culture compete for our attention and praise. We have to get into the "right school." We need to find the job that pays the most money. We attempt to carve our own path by sheer force of will. In the process, we may forget that God is the center of our attention and that loving others is a command of Christ. When success, money, and power are the most important things in our lives, then we will do anything to get them, even if it means losing ourselves. "They multiply their sorrows who court other gods," says the psalmist. We know in our hearts that nothing lasts forever, that fortunes can come and go in an instant. The psalmist trusts in the path that God lays out and in the counsel God gives. At no point does the psalmist talk about God's answer to his prayer. He simply affirms what he knows in his heart. God will not lead him astray. The Trappist monk Thomas Merton once wrote a prayer with a similar message. He said God would lead him on the right path, even if he knew nothing about it. Merton and the writer of Psalm 16 embraced the idea of God at the center of their lives and refused to let the world dictate who and what is most important. In doing so, they let go of the need for exact answers to accept what God had in store for them all along.

Prayer Action

Here I invite you to pray in four movements—with meditation on four lines of the psalm. Before you begin, read through the psalm aloud and allow the words you say to echo in your heart and mind. Find a time and space for prayer when you can spend some minutes in meditation. Quiet yourself and begin by simply breathing in and out.

Movement One: *Keep me safe, O God; in you I take refuge.*

Pray this line, breathing in on the first half and out on the second. When the rhythm is established, take a moment to name anything (and everything) that disturbs you, troubles you, challenges you, or makes you fearful in your life. Let these come without effort, and simply note them and lay them down. When you have named all you can, simply say, "From all that I have named and those things that are still in my heart, keep me safe, O God; in you I take refuge." Continue to breathe in and out until you feel the words are really a part of you.

Movement Two: *Lord, my allotted portion and my cup, you have made my destiny secure.*

As you continue to breathe, place God at the center of your life as a sacred inheritance from your family and faith community. If it is helpful, repeat the words "my portion and my cup" as you talk to God (or substitute your own understanding—words like *treasure, inheritance,* or *pearl*). When you have reminded yourself of God's importance as the center of your life, move to the second half of the verse: "You have made my destiny secure." Here allow every dream you have for your life to fall into God's hands. Do this for as long as it takes to let go of the need to control what happens. Repeat the psalmist's phrase and remind yourself that God will reveal your future when you are most ready for it.

Movement Three: *I bless the Lord who counsels me; even at night my heart exhorts me.*

Once again, breathe in on the first half of this verse and out on the second half. When you have taken the words into heart and mind, give yourself a chance to remember that God never stops talking to us. In books and people, through nature and dreams, morning and evening, the whispering voice of God lets us know he is near. Ask God for awareness and openness to divine counsel in your life. Invite God to speak to your heart so that, awake or asleep, you are in the Lord's presence. Return to the verse, breathing in and out.

Movement Four: *You will show me the path to life, abounding joy in your presence.*

As you continue your prayer, allow your breathing to accommodate this phrase, breathing in on the first half and out on the second. When you are relaxed and the words have become part of you, express confidence that God will show you the way. Ask God to make you so ready for the future he holds for you that when you see a path unfolding, you will not hesitate to embrace it. Do not deny the anxiety or occasional fear that occurs because you cannot see beyond the next bend. Rather, rest in the abounding joy of God's presence, which illuminates the path and will be there when we reach our destination. Return to your breathing and the words of the psalm. When you are finished, thank God for the graces of these words and the path he has shown you thus far.

> [Jesus said] "Do not let your hearts be troubled. You have faith in God; have faith also in me. In my Father's house there are many dwelling places. If there were not, would I have told you that I am going to prepare a place for you? And if I go and prepare a place for you, I will come back again and take you to myself, so that where I am you also may be. Where [I] am going you know the way." Thomas said to him, "Master, we do not know where you are going; how can we know the way?" Jesus said to him, "I am the way and the truth and the life. No one comes to the Father except through me. If you know me, then you will also know my Father. From now on you do know him and have seen him."
>
> John 14:1–7

Pause for Meditation

I used to think that prayer was about a specific answer to a specific question. In truth, Jesus recognizes that the needs we speak often hide the deeper needs of our heart. "Help me get an *A*" is often, "I m afraid of not measuring up." Thus God's answer is not always what we ask for, nor is God's direction always the one we would have chosen. Our lives unfold in God's hand a little at a time, sometimes maddeningly slow and sometimes in the blink of an eye. One of my former colleagues used to talk with college students and their parents about "long days and short years." I think our entire life is like that. We are children, and then before we know it, we are young adults, then those old people we used to wonder about. And we scarcely know how we got there.

This is what makes Jesus' teaching in John's Gospel so wonderful. He cuts right to the heart of the matter with his first words, "Do not let your hearts be troubled." Every deep question of our lives brings some anxiety. When we cannot ferret out an answer right away, we sense a restlessness until our path becomes clear to us. We invite and sometimes even demand answers from God, and we are often fairly clear what answer we are looking for. We are Thomas who wants the road laid out before him.

In the beginning of this teaching, Jesus is very clear. The many dwelling places of which he speaks not only have to do with room for anyone who wants to come but they have to do with the many directions by which we might get there. We do not need to know which path is the precise one nor do we need extremely specific answers on our way to where we are going. We do not have to know the destination. God has already revealed everything we need to know. Our path is where Jesus is; indeed, our path is Jesus himself. Knowing that, we can rest secure that whatever speed bumps, detours, scenic routes, and wrong turns we take, Jesus is there with us to guide our steps until we return home at last.

Prayer Action

Find a comfortable place and open your heart in silence to God. Read through the passage from John, aloud if possible, until the words become part of you. Imagine yourself at an intersection from which many roads radiate in different directions. For most of them, you can see only a few blocks until they curve around and out of sight. Breathe in and out as you consider each one, then find the park bench that is placed just off the intersection and go sit down.

Imagine Jesus coming to sit with you. Neither of you say anything at first, but you feel the peace of his presence and you trust that he is there for you. As you are able, talk about how it feels to be in the crossroads with him. With each breath, let go of any fear or anxiety about moving away from that place. Focus only on Jesus and let his calm bring you to the resting moment. When you have finished handing over your fear, your anxiety, and your need for exact answers, listen to him. "I am the way," he says. Repeat that phrase over and over in your memory until it becomes a part of you.

Imagine that you and Jesus stand up together and regard each road with a sense of calm. You are with the Lord who will not lead you down the wrong path. As you feel the peace of Jesus come over you, gradually come back to your prayer place. Reread the passage and thank God for the peace of Christ and for the path you are following now.

Prayer for Those Who Wonder Where They Are Going

Lord, Jesus Christ,
you moved with sure steps and godly confidence
from Nazareth to the Dead Sea to Caesarea Philippi
to Jerusalem to your death and you did not look back.

My way feels a little less sure.

Even now I look for certain answers and easy steps.

Or if the steps cannot be easy,
the knowledge that I am doing it (whatever *it* is) right.

You ask only that I trust in you,
that I let go of the need for a particular destination
and content myself with your path for my life.

So give me the grace to love the path
and to wonder at the twists and turns of my life,
both what is past and what is yet to come.

In your peace, may I find trust
that whatever I encounter will be with you.

And in the end, help me to know
that I will be where I started:
in your presence forever.

Amen.

Part III

Remembering God When We Wonder If We Will Ever Make a Difference

God calls all the souls he has created to love him with their whole being, here and thereafter, which means that he calls all of them to holiness, to perfection, to a close following of him and obedience to his will. But he does not ask all souls to show their love by the same works, to climb to heaven by the same ladder, to achieve goodness in the same way. What sort of work, then, must I do? Which is my road to heaven? In what kind of life am I to sanctify myself?

Blessed Charles de Foucauld
Originally published in *Cry the Gospel With Your Life*, reprinted 1999 by Orbis Books. Used with permission.

Chapter 8

We Learn and Teach in Every Place

The Question: How Will People Know I Was Here?

When I was on the admissions committee of the seminary in which I taught, I always asked prospective students what they hoped to learn from the seminary. They were usually very eloquent about what they needed to know and wanted to gain from their time there. Then I would ask what they had to teach the seminary. What would they leave behind? How would people know they had been there? They were far less sure of this answer, perhaps because no one had put the question to them in quite that way. While many students sat silent for a minute or two before they gave an answer, a few were able to talk about the passion they had for ministry. We could then have a conversation about being role models of learning and praying and about the practice of seeing ourselves as living examples of service to God and Church.

Many of us have been taught from early childhood not to think about what we bring to a situation. Rather, and particularly in our school years, the emphasis is placed on learning and receiving outside knowledge and skills. Rarely are we, as students or rookies, told that we have gifts to bring to the school, job, or home life that we share with others. This is a disservice. Both the brilliant student and the janitor who creates a welcoming environment have something to teach those they encounter in their daily routine. They, too, can shape the lives of those they meet. By the same token, both the greatest teacher and the most inexperienced student have something to learn from those they meet, and they are formed by them in more ways than can be counted.

Learning and teaching (like receiving and giving) are part and parcel of the Christian life. Learning keeps us humble before the miracle of God's creation and the diversity of humanity present before us. Learning is a celebration of intellect, curiosity, and imagination, all gifts of God. Everything we learn from any source molds us so that we can grow in wisdom before God. Teaching engages us in the joy of sharing ourselves with others—not just what we have learned, but what we have experienced, and what we think about, wonder at, and imagine. And somewhere deep inside we sense two things: we cannot teach well unless we know what it is to be a learner, and our learning finds its fruit only when we can teach someone else.

The joy of teaching and learning was evident in a group of sophomores charged with creating an evening of reflection for first-year students, whose entry into a highly competitive college atmosphere was often marked by anxiety and stress. For that evening, these four sophomore students designed an environment in which learning about one another became easy and comfortable, and sharing the insights of being a student and practicing faith was a highlight. The sophomores were the "experts" as far as the freshmen were concerned, but their openness to being shaped and touched by those whom they were leading made them companions on the journey. In truth, their teaching helped them reflect on the learning they had done as freshmen. And their openness to being taught by others helped everyone feel at ease during the time they spent together.

Almost all of us can name at least one great learning moment. One of mine came at the side of Sally, who had suffered with ALS for about three years. She had lost the ability to speak, but she could write haltingly on a chalkboard. When I first met her, she regaled me with tales of her childhood in Ireland and the adventures of a new life in America. Now I was visiting her to lend a little comfort as her physical health deteriorated. She was my teacher in her dying. Her eyes did not lose their sparkle. We talked about her funeral and what message she wanted to leave behind for people; and she could think only of the great pilgrimage home to God and the joy that awaited her. During our last visit a couple of days before she died, we embraced each other at the end, and she looked around at her sister standing in the kitchen and at me and, seemingly, at the whole world. She motioned for her chalkboard where she wrote, "I love you; I love you all." Sally had learned about love in her life. She taught what she learned throughout her life and powerfully in that moment. The difference she made in this world was etched on my face, on her sister's face, and on the faces of everyone who attended her funeral a few days later. In her living and dying, she had mastered the art of teaching and the humility of learning, and she never forgot that love was the foundation of both.

I hope all of us can name a great teaching moment as well. When we can impart a bit of wisdom, make a transition a little easier by sharing our experience and our empathy, then we will have made an impact that others will remember. It isn't always easy. What do we have that we can teach and share in a repetitive job or a class that we are required to take? What can we possibly bring to situations of disrespect or violence in which it seems all our learning has gone from us and we are left to wonder why we are there? The seminarians used to talk about growth opportunities and character builders. And it's true—we have much to learn from such situations. But let's stop to talk about why we might have been needed in those times. What could others have learned from us? What did we need to teach? What could we or did we give of ourselves so that all might leave a little more oriented toward grace and God? We cannot give our best selves to the next step in our lives unless we have taught and learned all we needed in the previous one. In such ways, God prepares us for something else and also works through us to teach others and influence them. It is God's way of helping us make a mark on the world.

The Resting Point: The Memory That God Wants Us to Learn and Teach

Meditate and pray through the memory using the following Scripture passages, and recall that God desires you to *teach others what you have learned.* Take your time and read the Scriptures aloud. Enhance your resting place by letting the meditation carry you into the prayer.

> Put on then, as God's chosen ones, holy and beloved, heartfelt compassion, kindness, humility, gentleness, and patience, bearing with one another and forgiving one another, if one has a grievance against another; as the Lord has forgiven you, so must you also do. And over all these put on love, that is, the bond of perfection. And let the peace of Christ control your hearts, the peace into which you were also called in one body. And be thankful. Let the word of Christ dwell in you richly, as in all wisdom you teach and admonish one another, singing psalms, hymns, and spiritual songs with gratitude in your hearts to God. And whatever you do, in word or in deed, do everything in the name of the Lord Jesus, giving thanks to God the Father through him.
>
> COLOSSIANS 3:12–17

Pause for Meditation

Nowhere in Paul's letters is the description of the attitude and behavior of the Christian so beautifully laid out as it is in the Letter to the Colossians. Paul draws attention immediately to the foundation of the transformed life. We are the beloved of God—God's own children, and as such, we are both a gift to one another and gifted by the presence of one another. Paul's exhortation is to honor God by honoring God's children wherever we find them.

Paul lays out particular ways to do that. Heartfelt compassion and kindness echo the "*hesed,*" or the steadfast love and mercy of God in the Old Testament, and the "*agape,*" or self-giving love of Jesus (who is God with us) in the New. Gentleness and patience remind us to see others with the mind of Christ. Only in this way can our hearts be turned toward the forgiveness that Christ has given us. Love, peace, and gratitude bind us together in the best of ways. And then Paul invites us to make a home for the word of Christ in our hearts. Remember how powerful the word of God is in the Old Testament. This word creates, sustains, and compels us to obedience. So it is with the word of Christ, whose teachings echo in our hearts as we continue to learn them day by day. Once we have learned from Christ, Paul exhorts us to teach and admonish one another, with praise and thankfulness for what we have learned in the first place. God teaches us what we need to know through Scripture, Tradition, and personal encounters. And God uses us to teach others until we are all ready for whatever is next.

Prayer Action

As you find your quiet place, allow your breathing to settle you down. With every breath you take, remind yourself that you are a beloved child of God. Ask God to be with you now and reveal how you have been a gift and how you have been gifted by others in your life. When you are as confident as you can be, remind yourself that God has both opened your heart to learn and also given you a heart to teach others.

Think over your life in the past year. Reflect on the many things you have learned. Who has helped teach those lessons? What did you learn and how will you carry it forward? Give thanks to God for working through these situations and these persons to teach you. Humbly ask God to continue forming you for the next part of your life.

Now reflect on the gifts you brought to the last year and on any ways in which you may have taught others. How did God work through you to teach others? What did someone else need that you were able to give? Remember that your teaching may plant seeds that come to great fruit later. You may have been exactly the person someone needed. In that moment, you were the image of Christ the teacher. Give thanks to God for the wisdom you were able to show and for the gifts you brought. Ask for the insight to see how these shaped you as well.

Your learning and your teaching have told you something about yourself and the ways in which you make a difference. Ask God for the humility to realize that you can never know it all and the confidence to share what little you have. Come back to your breathing and find yourself more and more open to your learning and your teaching in any situation. Bring your prayer to a close when you are ready.

> If you will give these instructions to the brothers, you will be a good minister of Christ Jesus, nourished on the words of the faith and of the sound teaching you have followed.... Command and teach these things. Let no one have contempt

for your youth, but set an example for those who believe, in speech, conduct, love, faith, and purity. Until I arrive, attend to the reading, exhortation, and teaching. Do not neglect the gift you have, which was conferred on you through the prophetic word with the imposition of hands of the presbyterate. Be diligent in these matters, be absorbed in them, so that your progress may be evident to everyone. Attend to yourself and to your teaching; persevere in both tasks, for by doing so you will save both yourself and those who listen to you.

1 Timothy 4:6, 11–16

Pause for Meditation

Paul's words to the young Timothy display his confidence in his protégé. He knows that since Timothy was a good learner, he will also be a good teacher, not just because of the things he teaches, but also because of the model he presents. Paul appreciates that we are readily influenced as much by the character of the one who teaches us as by the teachings themselves. What can we offer anyone if in our "speech, conduct, love, faith, and purity" we do not show ourselves to be transformed? Paul also reminds Timothy that even the young have something to teach the old.

Timothy's gift of teaching was given to him, but he must also be committed to continued learning: "Be diligent so that your progress may be evident…." In another letter to Timothy, Paul says, "Take as your norm the sound words that you heard from me, in the faith and love that are in Christ Jesus. Guard this rich trust with the help of the holy Spirit that dwells within us" (2 Timothy 1:13). Our learning encompasses more than mathematical equations or the hallmarks of Renaissance painting. Our true learning lifts us up, makes us excited, and opens up the possibilities of life to us. Our learning fosters the growth of our best selves. It reveals a little of the mystery of the world to us, and thus a little of the mystery of God.

In the same way, our teaching passes that revelation on to others in words and action. We can be old or young, well schooled or not, in a corporate office or a factory line, and what we have been given to learn will be unique to each of us, for we will grasp it as we are and it will affect us as much as we let it. What we teach and how we teach it reflect our learning, our openness, our humility, and our love. Together, our teaching and our learning may make an impact wherever we find ourselves and in whatever we do next.

Prayer Action

Before you begin to pray, take a little time to contemplate the words of faith that have nourished you. When and how did you first learn them? Who taught them to you? Bring those words and your teachers into your prayer today.

Invite God to be present, and when you are ready, read the Scripture aloud and listen to Paul tell you to set an example in your speech, conduct, love, faith, and purity for all those who believe. Listen as well when he exhorts you not to neglect the gift you have. Ask God to show you one or two times in which you were an example for others in any way. Who experienced you in this way? How did that happen?

When you have remembered the times you were an example, call to mind your teachers and invite them to see how you handed on what they nurtured in you. What are the "words of faith" that were particularly significant for you in your life? Offer all these memories, times, and people to God in thanksgiving.

Invite God to show you what you are learning right now from those around you. Even if nothing comes to mind, continue to ask God to reveal what you are teaching to others. What seeds are you leaving behind now?

Gently open yourself to the grace of learning and the courage to share what you learn with others. Close your prayer with the Lord's Prayer or another prayer of your choosing.

Prayer for Those Who Wonder What They Have to Give

My Lord Jesus,
we have one teacher, God alone,
who is the giver of all knowledge of the mind and heart.

In your Father's service you did not hesitate,
but opened your heart to learning
from parents and teachers in the Temple
and a Syrophoenician woman and others who followed you.

And at the same time you did not hesitate to teach
all who came to hear you
in love, in faithfulness, by word and example.

Give us the heart of a learner
that we may come to know your truth
in whatever way you choose to reveal it to us.

Give us the soul of a teacher
that we may share that truth by whatever means
you give us to do so and wherever you choose to send us.

And so will we praise and magnify you forever.

Amen.

Chapter 9

God Blesses the Journey

The Question: Am I There Yet?

In some ways this has been the hardest chapter to write, not because the ideas are difficult or complicated, but because I realize how much I look to the future to solve my problems and give me a chance to reinvent myself. How great it will be, we think, when we finally get to do what we want. I find this playing itself out in my preparation for vacations. I make lists, gather clothes and personal items, decide whether I want to bring a computer or a book (well, at least one book is a foregone conclusion, two is more likely). On the day of travel, I am eager to get to the airport or train station or into the car well ahead of the scheduled departure because I want the trip to start as soon as possible. When I arrive I am sure I will find myself with plenty of time and the wondrous possibilities of reading the book, having quiet dinners with friends and family, and catching up on sleep. I am sure my subconscious mind pictures me at my ideal best, freed from the cares of everyday life. Sometimes, it is hard for me to grasp that I am the same person, no matter how exotic the destination. My strengths remain my strengths and my "cutting edges" (the challenging moments or weaker sides of myself) are still in evidence. Even on vacation, the conversion of heart to which we are all called persists.

Vacations are not the only times we might say, "Things will be different once I get there." The "once I get there" takes many forms. "Things will be different when I lose ten pounds," we say. Or we pin our hopes on getting the degree or the ideal job or the spouse of our dreams because when that happens, we will be able to get things together and really make a difference. A professor at the university where I work often writes recommendations for students who want to apply to medical school. He once said, "When a student comes to ask for a recommendation to medical school, I ask him or her to tell me Plan B (the alternative if they do not make it). If they do not have a Plan B, I do not write them a recommendation." The students in the audience went slightly wide-eyed. Later he explained that a student who had only one plan in mind had not really explored their gifts or their possibilities. Going to medical school was not a free choice; it was a necessity. It was the only way they could define themselves. By contrast, someone who is free understands that the best they have to offer is not defined by a particular future plan but is present now and can be used in multiple ways. The student who "needed" to become a doctor would not make the best one.

I have thought about the professor often because I think he named a truth in our culture and in our lives. We are "destination people," always looking for the end point and believing that once we get there, we will automatically become the people we dream about. The trouble is, we want to name what that end point is and thus control it. The end point for us is often what society, culture, family, and friends tell us it is.

In the spiritual life, the destination is not nearly as important as the journey. The concept is "pilgrimage"—a journey to a holy place. On the pilgrim path, we don't reinvent ourselves or become new people; we discover who we were all along and that God has loved us from the first moment. We don't find God in the new land; we bring God with us and grow closer to him along the way. In this life our pilgrimage is clear. We come from God, we go home to God; and admission to this university, landing that job, or marrying that person does not mean we have finally made it. We are held in the hands of God, who watches our footsteps and brings us home by any of several roads.

As Christian disciples, we offer ourselves to God and in service to one another. There is nothing wrong with pursuing a particular career unless we think our happiness and God's can be found only if we succeed. The journey itself may change our path. Aspirations and dreams are good motivators, but God seeks our faithfulness right now while we are still on the way. Jesus once got into Simon Peter's boat and commanded Peter to put out into deep water. Peter hauled in such a mass of fish that he was overwhelmed. He fell to his knees and begged Jesus to get away from him because he was sinful. Jesus did not ask Peter to wait until he got himself together a little more. He did not ask about his business success or his home life. Jesus simply asked Peter to get up and follow him.

Jesus wanted Peter as he was in that moment—stubborn, sinful, passionate, eager, and willing. Those character traits didn't disappear when Peter was given the keys to the kingdom or when the Holy Spirit came upon him at Pentecost. But in his journey of faith, I think Peter came to understand that his life was not about the great amount of fish he would sell tomorrow or the reputation he would have ten years from now. Rather, he saw that discipleship was a daily encounter with the living Christ who asked for his full attention along the way and not in some particular and distant future. This is our resting point as well. If we do not know who we are now, we will not come to clarity on some distant shore. If we think things have to be different before we make a difference, we will miss the many opportunities to effect real change for ourselves and the world.

The Resting Point: The Memory That God Blesses the Journey

Meditate and pray through the memory using the following Scripture passages, and recall that God *is blessing you as you are in this present moment.* Take your time and read the Scriptures aloud. Enhance your resting place by letting the meditation carry you into the prayer.

How lovely your dwelling,
    O LORD of hosts!
My soul yearns and pines
    for the courts of the LORD.
My heart and flesh cry out
    for the living God.
As the sparrow finds a home
    and the swallow a nest to settle her young,
My home is by your altars,
    LORD of hosts, my king and my God!
Blessed are those who dwell in your house!
    They never cease to praise you.

Blessed the man who finds refuge in you,
    in their hearts are pilgrim roads.
As they pass through the Baca valley,
    they find spring water to drink.
    The early rain covers it with blessings.
They will go from strength to strength
    and see the God of gods on Zion.

LORD God of hosts, hear my prayer;
    listen, God of Jacob.
O God, watch over our shield;
    look upon the face of your anointed.

Better one day in your courts
than a thousand elsewhere.
Better the threshold of the house of my God
than a home in the tents of the wicked.
For a sun and shield is the LORD God,
bestowing all grace and glory.
The LORD withholds no good thing
from those who walk without reproach.
O LORD of hosts,
blessed the man who trusts in you!

PSALM 84

Pause for Meditation

Mother Teresa is quoted as saying that God does not ask us to be perfect, he asks us to be faithful. The psalmist sings his praise to the God of the journey, seeing the dwelling place of God at this moment and in the days to come. Even while he yearns for the fullness of the courts of the Lord, his soul finds refuge in the God of his life. This is faith that discovers its expression by trusting that God's path is better than anything the world could offer. In confidence, the psalmist expresses the glory of being in the presence of God and recognizes that there is one goal for human life, and that is to live with God forever by walking his path and giving praise to his name.

In the Scriptures, God looked for a faithful heart, not a perfect one. God desired his people to be humble and contrite in their sins and generous and available in their gifts. God did not ask that they take on this job rather than another or commit themselves to this person or community as opposed to another. Rather, God made a covenant with them and asked them to be God's people, whatever that might mean for the future. We are God's people now and, as the psalmist says, "in our hearts are pilgrim roads." If we commit ourselves to the journey, it will make all the difference.

Prayer Action

For all those who are on the pilgrimage of life, I would suggest you try walking while you pray. Before you begin, stretch and breathe in preparation for reflecting through your whole body. Read the psalm and bring it with you to keep rhythm while you walk. Invite God on the journey.

Allow the first line to echo in your heart as you go. "How lovely your dwelling, O LORD of hosts!" Imagine what that dwelling looks like and how it would feel to be there. In John's Gospel, Jesus tells those who believe that they already have eternal life. The psalmist talks about God's house as a present reality, where those who are there will never cease their praise. Praise God as you continue to imagine wandering throughout the house of the Lord.

Spend some time on the next verses. "Blessed the man who finds refuge in you, in their hearts are pilgrim roads." Pronounce that blessing on all your traveling companions and on yourself. And then ask, "What are my pilgrim roads?" Listen for the answer. As you continue in that stanza, ask yourself, "Where have I found spring water?" Name and lift up to God all those people and places who have been like spring water to you—refreshed you, rested you, and given you strength on your way.

Pray with the psalmist, "They will go from strength to strength." Name and lift up to God the strengths of character and grace that have been given to you in the past and in the present. If new ones have shown themselves, thank God for them. Humbly ask God for whatever strengths you might need for the future. Remember with the psalmist that the Lord withholds no good thing from those who trust in him. Breathe this part of the prayer in and out as you walk.

Give thanks for this resting point, and close the prayer with the Lord's Prayer or another prayer of your choosing. Return to your regular activities.

> The eleven disciples went to Galilee, to the mountain to which Jesus had ordered them. When they saw him, they worshiped, but they doubted. Then Jesus approached and said to them, "All power in heaven and on earth has been given to me. Go, therefore, and make disciples of all nations, baptizing them in the name of the Father, and of the Son, and of the holy Spirit, teaching them to observe all that I have commanded you. And behold, I am with you always, until the end of the age."
>
> MATTHEW 28:16–20

Pause for Meditation

Some fishermen, a tax collector, a physician, and assorted other people who thought they had arrived at the adult part of their lives gathered on a hilltop to hear Jesus tell them they hadn't reached their destination. The journey wasn't over yet. I can only imagine their thoughts. *Wait, I was settled...I had such plans...I like it here.* And while the mission was clear, Jesus was also maddeningly vague on the details. He didn't hold out to them a particular career, they were not given a blueprint for their lives nor a map with their destination (shades of Thomas!). Jesus didn't ask what further education they needed or if they could lose ten pounds before they started. He commissioned them as they were with their unique gifts and promised he would be with them to the very end. It must have felt like Plan B for all of them.

Still, they could start immediately, and both the commission and the promise would be a part of their lives throughout their journey. They would get used to being on the road and the changes of fortune they would find there. So it is with our lives and the command to use what we have for the sake of God, who gave all for us.

Prayer Action

Pilgrimage is not about leaving yourself behind nor believing everything will be fine once you get where you're going. Rather, it is living in this moment and taking your whole self into new situations, offering the best you have to give and knowing you will both shape and be shaped by whatever or whoever you meet there. In this prayer you will again use your imagination to become disciples who hear the call of Jesus to take everything they have been given by God and walk with sure steps into a future they do not know.

Find a comfortable seat in your favorite prayer space and quiet your heart and mind by breathing in and out rhythmically. Reread the passage from Matthew and invite Jesus to accompany you in your prayer.

Imagine yourself as the disciple whose life will be better when everything is in its place and you are settled once and for all. Now listen as Jesus gives you a new mission that may (or may not) take you in a different direction and tells you there will always be a new destination. Lay before Jesus the questions and concerns of your heart in the face of this. If you are tired of moving, tell him that; if you are eager to get to the end, tell him that as well.

Now open your heart and allow Jesus to give you a special grace for pilgrims. This is the grace of appreciating the gifts God has given you and finding a way to use them in every present moment. Allow this grace to fill you so fully that you understand that you do not have to wait for some future destination. Rather, you can be an instrument of God's love even now and in every place you find yourself.

Breathe out your thanks and ask Jesus to continue to be present to you throughout your life, especially when you begin to think that you will have to wait to accomplish his mission for you.

Prayer for Those Who Wonder If They Are There Yet

Lord, I thought I was comfortable where I was
or at least I knew what to expect.

But I have been so restless lately,
wondering if a change of scenery
might mean a change of heart
and feeling as if I have to get there to know for sure.

But you have come again, naming my desire to be with you
and calling me to welcome where I am
even as I move into an unexpected, unknown future.

I am not always content to do that.

I do not always understand
that you want the person I am now
as well as the person I will be.

I have a hard time believing
that your dwelling place is everywhere
and that I can ask you anything—even to be my savior.

I do not have to wait until I am perfect.

Is it any wonder, then, that on this road, in this place,
I feel a peculiar peace
that might be the companionship of fellow travelers
or your holy presence at my side.

So let me slow my walk just a little
or even stop to take in the scenery,
to breathe in grace and the love of God
and remember them in every place I am.

Amen.

Chapter 10

The God of Our Whole Life

The Question: Why Can't I Be in Control of My Own Life?

Two stories in Scripture evoke great response in almost every conversation I have, whether the person is in college, in a job or career, or finding the next step in middle age or in retirement. The first is from the Book of Daniel (5:1–30) when the hand of God appears to King Belshazzar and writes on the wall and Daniel is summoned to interpret the handwriting. The second is from the Acts of the Apostles (9:1–22) when Saul (later Paul) is thrown to the ground, struck blind, and hears the voice of Jesus asking, "Saul, Saul, why are you persecuting me?" In both instances, the conversation turns not on the principal themes of the narrative, but on two other issues. The first is the way in which the message is delivered to the recipients. "I wish it were that easy," people say. "I would love to have handwriting on the wall or a bolt from the blue. Things would be so much clearer. I would know exactly what to do." The second is the clarity with which each main character understands his mission in life. Daniel's clear gift of interpretation will help Belshazzar know exactly where he stands with God. Paul takes on his mission to the Gentiles with eagerness. The difference they made was astounding.

Our desire for handwriting on the wall and clear voices, visions, and missions says a great deal about our uneasiness with uncertainty and our desire to control what is coming and how we play a part in it. If I know what I'm going to do, I can get there faster, do it longer, and be better at it. I will make the right choices and, with laserlike focus, choose the difference I will make in the world and in my life. If we have control we will not be caught off guard. We will know exactly what to do, and we will live the life we want without surprises. Our need for control often leads to our greatest temptations and is certainly one of the many occasions for sin in contemporary society.

Control, in and of itself, is not a bad thing. We tell children to control themselves when they are running wild, and we try to control our appetites, our impulses for pleasure, and the temptation to stay on the couch and watch a full season of our favorite TV show in one sitting. But when our need to control drives us to manipulate situations and people for our gain, we have lost perspective. When our need to control the future means we refuse to consider any option other than the one we have chosen for ourselves, then we have closed ourselves off to the multiple ways in which God might call us to service through our talents, gifts, and work. Wanting control is often behind our desire to make money and get ahead. When that becomes the only thing we want, it might be time to reexamine what is really important to us and to live open to the possibilities God might have in mind.

As an antidote to our control, the theology of church and synagogue articulates the notion that God is the ruler of all. "God reigns" is the cry of the psalmist. Jesus is called "king" and "Lord." The great Jewish leader Abraham Heschel once said that to pray is to invite God to intervene in our lives and become the master of our souls. If we mean what we say, then we must let go of the need to know exactly what is going on or how God will use us.

We have to hand over our desire to "control the outcome." Rather, we allow God to unfold our lives before us, and we live with some uncertainty about God's future plans.

Frequently this comes up in conversations about vocations of all sorts. "I know God wants me to be married," someone will say. "I can't be called to religious life because I don't want to be celibate," another will chime in. Those things may be true, but we cannot know with exact accuracy what God wants because handwriting on the wall is so rare. Cutting off the possibilities because we don't think we will like the answer or because we want to avoid the perceived cost is one of the things that keeps us from being vulnerable to God's reign in our lives. It tells God that something else might be ruling us.

In Jesus' time, the disciples argued over who was the greatest and told Jesus that his crucifixion and death could not happen. Clearly, they did not always order their lives around God's will. They made their own need for control evident. But following Christ is an invitation to uncertainty. Jesus commanded his disciples to wish the peace of God on any house they entered, sit at the kitchen table, and eat what was put in front of them (one of the hardest commands in the Bible). How much more uncertain could they get? But how else could they (or we) encounter every person where they live and know their anxieties as well as their joys? Jesus didn't tell the disciples they needed to heal the sick, cast out demons, or prophesy. He did tell them they needed to take up their cross, which expressed their willingness to let go of everything—even their own lives if necessary—for the sake of the reign of God. He told them to preach the Good News wherever they found themselves, but he gave no specifics about how they were to do that. I am sure the disciples experienced days of great frustration when the path they were on seemed completely obscure. "What are we doing this for?" they must have asked many times.

But in every place where people have followed the invitation of Christ rather than their own desires, the poor have been fed, the oppressed freed, and the sick cared for. Children and adults have been taught, peace has been championed, and the dignity of all people before God has been promoted. All of this has happened in ways that honored the gifts and passions of each disciple who chose to follow in the first place. Our resting point here is the recognition that if we stop trying to determine and control the outcome of our lives and start allowing God to direct us, we too will make a difference no matter how mundane our lives may seem.

The Resting Point: The Memory That God Reigns

Meditate and pray through the memory using the following Scripture passages, and recall that *God reigns eternally.* Take your time and read the Scriptures aloud. Enhance your resting place by letting the meditation carry you into the prayer.

> When they had finished breakfast, Jesus said to Simon Peter, "Simon, son of John, do you love me more than these?" He said to him, "Yes, Lord, you know that I love you." He said to him, "Feed my lambs." He then said to him a second time, "Simon, son of John, do you love me?" He said to him, "Yes, Lord, you know that I love you." He said to him, "Tend my sheep." He said to him the third time, "Simon, son of John, do you love me?" Peter was distressed that he had said to him a third time, "Do you love me?" and he said to him, "Lord, you know everything; you know that I love you." [Jesus] said to him, "Feed my sheep. Amen, amen, I say to you, when you were younger, you used to dress yourself and go where you wanted; but when you grow old, you will stretch

out your hands, and someone else will dress you and lead you where you do not want to go." He said this signifying by what kind of death he would glorify God. And when he had said this, he said to him, "Follow me."

John 21:15–19

Pause for Meditation

Some have called this story the "mid-life" gospel as it so eloquently points out the freedom we feel when we are young and the need to follow a different call when we grow older. I think it is "living word" for all those who wonder what to do next or how they will make a difference in this life. It is also a reminder that we do not always control what happens to us. All we can do is respond to the questions of Jesus and allow him to show us what this means.

One key in this Scripture lies in the asking and answering of the three questions. Jesus does not ask, "Will you do me a favor?" He asks from the bottom of his heart if Peter loves him. Only in a context of love given and received can Jesus request, "Feed my sheep." The flock is a shepherd's most precious possession. It gives him purpose and meaning. No shepherd would leave the care of his flock in the hands of someone he did not love or trust.

The second key for this Scripture is Jesus' metaphor for the spiritual life: When we make a commitment to love the Lord, we move from going where we want to going where he leads us. Here, more than almost anywhere, Jesus expresses to us that our lives are in God's hands, and his final command to Peter to "follow me" is an invitation to let God reign in our lives and do for the flock what Jesus did—helping to bring them safely home.

Today, Jesus asks us, "Do you love me?" The answer often

comes unhesitatingly. We do love Jesus, or we think we should love Jesus and it's the right thing to say. What we may not realize is that Jesus takes our answer at face value and prepares to hand over his flock, which includes every person we love, those we don't, and those whom we have not yet met. In love and trust, Jesus asks us to care for the flock and to follow him to the cross into the glory of his resurrection. How do we make a difference? We do it by placing Jesus at the center of our lives as teacher and master. We do it by remembering what Jesus asks us to do every day. We do it first by loving Christ and then seeing where love leads us as we care for those whom Jesus has entrusted to us.

Prayer Action

I invite you to use this as an examination of conscience. To begin, let go of every worry about where your life is going and how you will make your mark. Enter into a quiet place in your heart and mind. If it helps to take some deep breaths, do so.

Invite Jesus to be with you. As you sit with the Lord, turn attentively to him. He has something he wants to ask you.

"[Insert your name here], do you love me more than these?" Jesus asks. For a minute, think about all the silly things in your life that keep you from living in a faithful way. For some, that might be too much time spent on the Internet or in front of the television. It might be a real craving for food or more fun than usual. Answer, "Yes, Lord, you know I love you." When Jesus responds and asks you to feed his sheep, ask yourself, *What does that mean here?* How easy would it be to give those things up if it meant you could feed the sheep better?

The second time Jesus asks the question, think about the habits of thought or behavior that make it difficult at times to respond to someone in your life with love. These are the things that make it a little harder to answer Jesus. But still we come back saying, "Yes, Lord, you know I love you." When Jesus quietly asks us to tend his sheep, ask what it might mean for the flock if we had the grace to change these habits just a little. How would we be more faithful and better able to care for Jesus' sheep?

When Jesus asks his final question, bring to mind the deep wounds and scars from which most of our sins spring. These are often hidden fears, beliefs, and anger that derail us at unexpected moments. They are so much a part of us that it is often hard to give them up because we do not know how to live without them. In some ways, they may make us say to Jesus, "Can I get back to you on that?" Still, we may love Jesus in spite of those deep fears. How can we let go of any of those things? Can you ask for the healing that would make it possible to feed Jesus' sheep, and what would that look like? When you have finished listening to Jesus' three questions, offer to the Lord all the things that came to mind and ask for healing and forgiveness so that you can be free to do his will.

Recall the second half of the reading and either physically or mentally lift your arms to allow Jesus to fasten his belt around you and take you to the next place on your journey. Recognize that you will have to die to many of the things you named in the first half of the meditation to follow him. But also remember that you love him and that he loves you and has given over the care of his flock to you in the name of love. He will not leave you alone to face your dangers.

Breathe deeply and thank God for the love and forgiveness he has shown through Jesus. Place Christ at the center of your life as the one who loves you, directs you, and walks with you now and into the future. Allow yourself to be led by him and hear him trust you to do his work. Acknowledge before the Lord that you do not need to see his future for you because you can serve him as his disciple now.

> "Come to me, all you who labor and are burdened, and I will give you rest. Take my yoke upon you and learn from me, for I am meek and humble of heart; and you will find rest for yourselves. For my yoke is easy, and my burden light."
>
> MATTHEW 11:28–30

Pause for Meditation

An English hymn, "I Heard the Voice of Jesus Say," takes its inspiration from this text. The author is nineteenth-century writer Horatius Bonar, and one line reads, "I came to Jesus as I was, weary and worn and sad; I found in him a resting place, and he has made me glad." I know of no one who does not hope that he or she will make a mark on this world. In fact, most of the students I know long to change the world for the better. They want to do good and do it well. Like many students, they take double and triple majors. They also take on extracurricular assignments where they can tutor, mentor, or serve those who have not had the same opportunities. I know people who hold down two jobs so they can house and feed their families and who will be among the first to lend a helping hand to a neighbor in need. The mark they leave is not always seen, nor will they necessarily be known beyond the church, school, or neighborhood in which they live. The questions they ask (along with all of us) are good: "What have I done?" and "Have I done the best I could?" But we also need to recognize that the desire to make a difference cannot be driven by the need to be the savior of the world. When that happens, we refuse to say "no" and begin to make our desires the only things that matter. Instead, serving the world must be grounded first in the love of Christ and in gratitude for what Christ has done for us.

Into this temptation to help everyone, Jesus offers himself as a resting point for our worries and cares as well as whatever need drives us to take on more and more until we have nothing left to give. Jesus gently turns us from the needs that drive us to cling to our own power and, instead, invites us to place our trust in him. We cannot, by sheer force of will, make things happen, avoid suffering, or create happiness. In the end there is only the love of God, in which we rest and through which we can love as Christ loved.

Prayer Action

This lovely Scripture from Matthew is calming in and of itself. Find your quiet space in your room, house, chapel, or outside. Prepare for your prayer by asking God's blessing and inviting Jesus to reveal his living presence to you.

Slowly begin reading this Scripture, pausing often to allow the words of Christ to warm, invite, console, and live in you. Listen as Christ says, "Come to me...and I will give you rest." Repeat those words as a mantra while you relax your body, mind, and heart. If some other thought intrudes, gently take it to Jesus, knowing that you do not have to carry it at this moment. Listen again as Jesus invites you to take his yoke and learn from him. The love and the mission of the Lord are born in a humble heart, which seeks only to do the will of the Father. When we are grounded in that, as Jesus was, we too can fulfill our mission, whatever it might be, and do so for the greater glory of God rather than for ourselves.

Jesus repeats that we will find rest for ourselves, and so repeat that to yourself, allowing it to fill your heart and mind with peace. With each repetition, let your whole being rest against the Lord. Allow him to dispel fear so you can give your life to him. When you have rested as much as you can, begin to thank the Lord for the grace of rest and freedom from the need to control how you will make a difference. Instead, embrace the peace of Christ that surrounds you and resolve to carry that into the world.

When you are ready, pray a closing prayer of your choosing and return to your day.

Prayer for Those Who Wonder Why They Can't Be in Control

God, Ruler of my heart; God, Lord of my life;
God, Savior of the world,
I sometimes find it difficult to let go
and let you be in charge of my life.

I have so much to do and see so much that needs to be done
that occasionally I forget that I am not the one
who can do it all.

There are days when I feel like I have made
no difference at all
because I cannot see seeds that are planted
or lives that were touched for only five minutes.

That is when I begin to force myself beyond my capacity
and insert myself into others' lives, asking for attention,
not for your glory, but for myself and what I need.

Bring me, Lord, to that place of rest
where I know you as the ground of my being,
where I allow you to show me the path of your choosing,
and where, rooted and grounded in your love,
I can be content to find my purpose in your will.

Amen.

Chapter 11

Called to Be Holy Everywhere

The Question: How Can I Possibly Be Holy?

Nina was middle-aged when I first met her. She was one of those wisdom figures you don't forget easily. In the turbulent sixties and in the wake of the Second Vatican Council, she opened a bookstore that became a gathering place for Catholics who celebrated great conversations and embraced the apostolate of the laity. I was young when I first walked into the store and found a treasure house of great books, great art, and conversation. I was a bit older when I met her the second time. By then she had lived a lifetime of faith and had definite opinions about some Church matters while her devotion to living out her baptismal calling continued to be evident. We had several conversations that were always enlightening and usually full of laughter.

One of the most memorable was her recollection of Dorothy Day, who had been a good friend until her death in 1980. I don't recall many details from their early friendship, but I will never forget the story Nina told about the time spent working in a Catholic Worker House like the one Day cofounded in New York. Nina recalled that she had been inspired by Dorothy's work and wanted with all her heart to join her in the great enterprise. To her great dismay, she got to the end of her time and said, "I realized this was not my calling. What Dorothy was doing was wonderful, but I was called to a different path." She turned that passion into support, not only for the Catholic Worker Houses, but for social movements designed to root out injustice and promote peace in the world. Many people talk about the gospel; she lived it. She died in 2007 at the age of ninety-two, ready to meet the God for whom she had labored so faithfully in the vineyard.

I tell the story of Nina to hone in on the last thing that gets in the way of our making a difference in the world. After we have become comfortable with the idea of pilgrimage and bringing our whole being to bear in each moment, after we have let go of the need to be in control of our future and our lives, we come finally to tackle the anxiety or questioning that happens when we realize we may not be the one who rushes into the burning building or lives among the urban poor or gives an entire life as a missionary in another country. I do not say this as an easy excuse to abandon our gospel call. Rather, I say it to remind us that our mission is not always tied to the spectacular gestures and the biggest ideas. In every day and in every way, our mission is to be holy "because the Lord, our God is holy."

Scripture tells us that the word *holy* means "to set apart." Holy people and holy nations are set apart as God's own in this world and hold themselves to a different standard than the world might offer. We often have difficulty even thinking of ourselves in this way. Holiness, we think, is the province of the saint; unattainable by mere human beings. For some, holiness means praying for hours on end or giving up one's life for one's faith. But God made us to be in his image, and at its heart, holiness is the embrace of our identity as the image of God. How we live in and through that image will make our holiness evident to all we meet. We cannot look at Mother Teresa or Dorothy Day and say, "I am not doing that, therefore I am not holy." Nor can we say, "Holiness is only for people who do what they have done." On the contrary, holiness is the occupation of all of us, whether we are in a bookstore, a soup kitchen, or on the streets of Calcutta.

Sometimes, we connect holiness with the official ministers who serve the Church. This is another way of avoiding the responsibility. When God chose to become one of us in Jesus, he showed us what holiness was and could be for us. We are the image of God every day. We are called to be holy every day. How we "do" holiness depends on the circumstances in which we find ourselves, the gifts we have been given, and the passions that will shape our gifts for the sake of the kingdom of God.

While we may not think of ourselves as set apart or ordained, our ministries carry in them the original meaning of serving at the table and then go back further to the root that means "to do the lesser things." The washing of feet, the drying of tears, caring for the elderly parent or the sick child, offering a greeting or a gesture of concern to someone who is troubled—these are all part and parcel of being a minister and being holy in all places and times. Doing the lesser things is not just how we minister, it is how we embrace our identity as the image of God. The holy life is life lived as a disciple of Christ in offices, schoolyards, dorm rooms, neighborhoods and any other place the people of God call home. It is a life worthy of the image of God. Like the drip of water that erodes the rock, each moment in which we practice being holy changes us over time until we show forth the glory of God in all we do.

When we get to thinking that our lives are less worthy because we haven't done the spectacular work someone else has done, then we have abandoned the idea of being holy because we are the image of God and have started to think of holiness as a competition. *Who can do it better and what can I do to win?* Such an attitude kills the spirit because we will either find ourselves wanting and feel guilty or think we are superior and become self-centered, concerned only with how we look to others. Nina did not compete for a "holiness" prize with Dorothy Day. She found her own path that allowed her to do the small things for every person she met. When we are wondering how or if we have made a difference, we might ask ourselves, "How have I been holy today?" and remember that God created us in his image to follow his path, no matter how small our steps may seem.

The Resting Point: The Memory That God Calls Us to Be Holy

Meditate and pray through the memory using the following Scripture passages, and recall that God *uniquely calls you to holiness.* Take your time and read the Scriptures aloud. Enhance your resting place by letting the meditation carry you into the prayer.

> When the Son of Man comes in his glory, and all the angels with him, he will sit upon his glorious throne, and all the nations will be assembled before him. And he will separate them one from another, as a shepherd separates the sheep from the goats. He will place the sheep on his right and the goats on his left. Then the king will say to those on his right, "Come, you who are blessed by my Father. Inherit the kingdom prepared for you from the foundation of the world. For I was hungry and you gave me food, I was thirsty and you gave me drink, a stranger and you welcomed me, naked and you clothed me, ill and you cared for me, in prison and you visited me." Then the righteous will answer him and say, "Lord, when did we see you hungry and feed you, or thirsty and give you drink? When did we see you a stranger and welcome you, or naked and clothe you? When did we see you ill or in prison, and visit you?" And the king will say to them in reply, "Amen, I say to you, whatever you did for one of these least brothers of mine, you did for me." Then he will say to those on his left, "Depart from me, you accursed, into the eternal fire prepared for the devil and

> his angels. For I was hungry and you gave me no food, I was thirsty and you gave me no drink, a stranger and you gave me no welcome, naked and you gave me no clothing, ill and in prison, and you did not care for me." Then they will answer and say, "Lord, when did we see you hungry or thirsty or a stranger or naked or ill or in prison, and not minister to your needs?" He will answer them, "Amen, I say to you, what you did not do for one of these least ones, you did not do for me." And these will go off to eternal punishment, but the righteous to eternal life.
>
> MATTHEW 25:31–46

Pause for Meditation

Matthew's end-of-the-world judgment scene may seem like an odd choice for a resting point. It seems more frequently used as an examination of conscience or a preparation for end-time sermons. What we want to remember, though, is that our resting points are times of attentiveness, allowing us to be ready to move in any direction. This passage highlights two things that help us in our attentiveness. The first is the generosity of the sheep who did the small things as they needed to be done, not because they saw Christ, but because the acts came to them as naturally as breathing. "How can I repay the Lord for all the great good done for me?" asks the psalmist (116:12). Behind that question is this one: "By God's holiness and love, I have come to this place. How can I do any differently?"

The answer was not found in strict adherence to ritual to the exclusion of pastoral care and love of others—nearly all the prophets preached about the transformation of heart that marked someone who had truly heard the Lord's voice. To care for the widows and orphans and all who were marginalized was the beginning of obedience to God and a means of returning the good the Lord had done. Jesus pushes us even further in his preaching to enter a relationship of love with all people. We are to become the human face of God's love for all we meet. It does not matter whether we see Christ in them. We reach out in love because of the love we have been given. In this way, inch by inch, in small and large ways, we become holy as God is holy.

The second resting point is Jesus' emphasis on the least of these little ones. Sometimes we are so busy looking for the big things we can do to grow in holiness that we miss the little everyday things. In the ministry in which I work, we have enormously generous young and old adults who put together valentine kits for the local children's hospital, go on alternative break trips for service both in and out of the country, and cook and serve at the local soup kitchen every Sunday. Still, there is not a community gathering that goes by that I don't see one or more students, newcomers, or strangers standing alone, wondering who is going to welcome them in. I don't say this to indict those who are already serving in different capacities, but to point out how the road to holiness doesn't have to be in Nicaragua or New Orleans; it can start right next to us. We have somehow become accustomed to thinking we have to wait until the big moment comes before we can start growing in the holiness and love of God. The smallest gesture of love done for the least of people is done for Jesus. Jesus' words compel us to live into ourselves as the image of God whether we follow the path of Dorothy Day or the path of Nina Moore.

Prayer Action

The resting point in this Scripture is not so much the eternal rest or punishment of God but, rather, the invitation to find the little ways we can practice being holy. If you find it helpful, bring a notebook and pencil into your prayer and write down names of people who come to your mind and place them before your eyes and God's.

Find your comfortable place and invite God to be present to you. When you are ready, give praise to God for the love he has shown you. Know that you are created in the image of God. Humbly ask God for the grace to be holy as he is holy, in small and large ways, and ask God to show you where you might do that today.

Read through the Scripture once slowly, then go back to the words of Jesus for both sheep and goats. Begin to think of each phrase/action in a very broad sense. As people come to your mind, write down their names if it is helpful.

> *"For I was hungry and you gave me food, I was thirsty and you gave me drink..."*

Are there people in your life now who are physically hungry or thirsty? How can you feed their bodies? Can you take them to the grocery store, invite them to dinner, or simply share a snack or a drink with them? This might be the elderly couple on your street, the student studying for exams, or the homeless man or woman in your town.

Are there some who are emotionally hungry or thirsty? What are they hungry or thirsty for? Is it companionship, a sense of belonging, a need to know that someone cares? Do they need to tell their story or talk about what is happening in their lives? How can you feed them today? Think about nursing-home residents, a mother with a newborn, a neighbor who just moved in, or a student who is new at school. They all want to be known by somebody in their lives.

Are there some in your life who are hungry for knowledge? Do they need help in school or in learning a skill? Do they just want to pick your brain about something? This might be a child who needs tutoring, a young adult who would love to learn your skill at gardening or woodworking. Can you feed them today?

"…a stranger and you welcomed me, naked and you clothed me…"

Who is the stranger in your life? Is it the eccentric woman in your neighborhood, the classmate who doesn't know anyone, the new family in your church? Maybe it's the child or adult who has a disability or the person who always seems to be alone. How will you welcome this stranger?

Nakedness is another name for shame and embarrassment and feeling exposed to the stares of others. It comes in many forms. Who is the naked person for you? Is he or she the butt of a joke, the person who fell, or the acquaintance who committed a great *faux pas* in front of friends? How might you clothe them with your words, kindness, or willingness to look past their behavior to model what love looks like?

"…ill and you cared for me, in prison and you visited me…"

Who in your school, church, or neighborhood is ill in body, mind, or spirit? What does caring look like for them? Is it as simple as bringing Communion to the sick, giving a seat to someone who has need of it, or reaching out to someone or the family of someone who is depressed?

Prisons are not always marked by bars. We see them in the faces of those who deal with the addictions of loved ones and those who are abused. Anyone who feels trapped in a life not of their choosing is in prison. We cannot always help in immediate and effective ways, but their stories are no less compelling, and prisoners have great need to tell others about their lives. Who in your life is in a prison of sorts? What can you do to visit them?

As you finish your meditations, reflect on the people whose names you wrote down or remembered. We practice being holy by loving and caring for them as God does. Give thanks to God for revealing them to you and showing you that holiness comes in loving them as you love him.

Let love be sincere; hate what is evil, hold on to what is good; love one another with mutual affection; anticipate one another in showing honor. Do not grow slack in zeal, be fervent in spirit, serve the Lord. Rejoice in hope, endure in affliction, persevere in prayer. Contribute to the needs of the holy ones, exercise hospitality. Bless those who persecute [you], bless and do not curse them. Rejoice with those who rejoice, weep with those who weep. Have the same regard for one another; do not be haughty but associate with the lowly; do not be wise in your own estimation. Do not repay anyone evil for evil; be concerned for what is noble in the sight of all. If possible, on your part, live at peace with all. Beloved, do not look for revenge but leave room for the wrath; for it is written, "Vengeance is mine, I will repay, says the Lord." Rather, "if your enemy is hungry, feed him; if he is thirsty, give him something to drink; for by so doing you will heap burning coals upon his head." Do not be conquered by evil but conquer evil with good.

ROMANS 12:9–21

Pause for Meditation

If being holy has to do with living into our identity as the image of God, Paul's frequent prescriptions for the Christian life give us the practical applications of what that means. Paul was clear that baptism was transformative. As disciples of Christ, we turn away from that which is not of God and turn toward lives that proclaim the holiness of the Lord and our desire to enter this life. For Paul, this touches every aspect of our lives, as this passage shows. God's call to holiness is not something exotic, to be worked at as we have the time or opportunity. The essence of Christian life is that we practice holiness in every encounter. Then little by little, through the help and grace of God, we help make the world holy.

What I love about this passage is the thoroughness and the injection of a very human sentiment. Love, rejoicing, service, hospitality, peace, and compassion are all paths to holiness. When Paul echoes the words of Matthew at the end, he cannot help but insert that little human emotion. Even feed your enemies because, it seems, it will just make them crazy. I am paraphrasing, of course, but Paul reminds us that we are complex beings and that we often do the right things for the wrong reasons. If it results in forming us in holiness, then, Paul seems to think, do it anyway. By being holy we can conquer evil.

Prayer Action

Use this Scripture as a starting point. Read it through aloud once or twice, and then put it aside and enter your prayer space. Welcome God into the space with you and rejoice in his presence. Invite God to uncover your paths to holiness as you pray.

Gently recall the passage and pause when the first phrase, whatever it is, enters your mind. As an example, take "If possible, live at peace with all." Allow yourself to review the past day for places where the peace of God was manifest in you and where it was not. If you were able to be at peace, particularly in the presence of others, thank God for the opportunity to practice holiness. If you were irritated or anxious for any reason, ask God for the grace to take that step to holiness in the days to come.

Repeat this process as many times as you like. When you are finished, pray for the courage to embrace the quest for holiness. Ask for the grace to see the smallest moments in which being holy will matter so that when the larger opportunities present themselves, you may be found ready and willing to be the image of God then as well. Might that set you apart from the world? Yes, but it also gives the world another example of what it means to be holy. Close your prayer in thanksgiving and praise of God and in whatever other way seems appropriate.

Prayer for Those Who Wonder If They Can Be Holy

Good and gracious God,
you alone are Lord and you alone are holy,
except that you made us in your image
and called us to be holy like you.

We can never be holy exactly like you,
but we can be the image of you that others see.

We may give our lives in service of the poor
or spend our time in a country not our own.

We may greet the stranger in our community
or buy a cup of coffee because someone
is thirsty for friendship
and to know they are a child of God.

We may start a "Catholic Worker" house
or simply work at being Catholic,
trying to love, serve, rejoice, and care for others
as Jesus cared for them.

In all these steps, large and small, we grow in holiness,
we help make the world holy,
until at last we grow into oneness with you.

Help us grow into oneness with you;
God and the image of God—one forever and ever.
Amen.

Conclusion

In this amazing, complex, crazy expedition we call life, questions and answers about identity, direction, and meaning enter our minds and hearts in both subtle and not-so-subtle ways. They come as old friends, unwelcome guests, or total strangers. They linger helpfully or loiter maddeningly. They can compel us to action or exhaust us with choices. We devote time and energy to finding correct answers and even more correct paths to follow or we ignore them, hoping they will go away and leave us in the current trajectory—which may not be great, but at least we know what it is.

Into the midst of the questions and the business of living, the Lord comes with steadfast love and abiding mercy. He comes to comfort, to challenge, to call, to push, to prod, and to urge us on as disciples of Christ and children of his own heart. The Lord comes as the gentle ruler of our heart and the vision that is ever before us. In the wonderful tradition from which we come, the memories of our relationship with God emerge in stories, sermons, prophecies, prayers, parables, and conversation. But the world sometimes intrudes on those memories, and the noise of our wondering, our needs, and our fears occasionally makes us hard-of-hearing. It becomes easy to miss a still, small voice when so much is going on.

"Come to the zero point and rest," my long-ago teacher said when we had finished a dance exercise. We dutifully took up our neutral first position and waited, ready to move when we were asked to do so and able to move wherever she wanted us to go. My teacher knew the value of those moments of relief that gave tired muscles and tired minds a chance to recover and find renewed energy for movement. We have the same need in our spiritual life. "Come to your resting point," says the Lord as we stretch and wrestle with the questions in our lives. "Come to balance, come to attentiveness, come to the place from which you can move in any direction as soon as you hear the command." The resting point is not about giving up or giving in; it simply allows the space and time for hearts, souls, and minds to stop their ceaseless wandering and wondering and breathe for a minute.

While writing this book, I had to make use of many resting points because anxiety and stress are the enemies of forward motion. In the two years since I first began, I have experienced my own need for control over my life, my own desire for clarity and direction, the belief that I have little to offer, and the regular (seemingly incessant) question of who I am as I approach the latter half of my life. I have started, and I have stopped. I have embraced some of the changes the questions bring and have stubbornly resisted others. In short, I have been human. In the process, I have found the truth about our spiritual resting points. They appear when we *remember God,* whether that is in the beauty of creation or reflecting on the imagination, variety, and order of the universe. We remember God in conversations with friends—face-to-face with someone who loves us, tells us the truth, and reminds us that God's love started it all—and there is a resting point. We remember God in the silence of hearts broken open so that God's whispering voice can make itself heard above the noise outside—another resting point. We remember God in the stories told in the words of prophets, psalmists, letter writers, and Jesus himself, who is God come to earth. Each and every one of these is another God-memory in which we can pause and come to balance, and from there be up and off and on our way to heaven, no matter which direction he takes us.